Setan's baptism in Khao I Dang Refugee Camp / Thailand

MIRACLES IN THE FORGOTTEN LAND AND BEYOND

THE STORY OF SETAN AND RANDA LEE'S LIFE
FROM THE KILLING FIELDS OF CAMBODIA
TO THEIR MIRACULOUS ONGOING
MISSION WORK IN THEIR HOMELAND

**Setan and Randa Lee
with Shelba Hammond**

God bless

[signature]

[signature]

This book is dedicated to
Setan Lee's father,

Mr. Chan Lee
February 5, 1920 - August 7, 2010

My Tribute to Dad
Chan Lee

꧁꧂

Dad, you are my hero. Therefore, I dedicate this book to you. In all that I have done and will do, if not for you and our Almighty God, I would not be the person I am today. You inspired me with your love, your actions and your incredible example of the love of God. Your compassion for your kids, grandkids, great grandkids, and your friends has influenced all of our lives tremendously. Moreover, Dad, you always taught me to do "life service, not lip service." Your encouragement for me to love others has been so ingrained in me and you have seen it so evidenced in my life. Our Lord Jesus spoke in His word, *"Love the Lord your God with all your heart and with all your soul and with all your mind and with all your strength.' The second is this: 'Love your neighbor as yourself.' There is no commandment greater than these." Mark 12:30-31* (NIV)

One other important item that you always taught me was, "if you want anyone to trust you and put investments into your work, you must first prove yourself to them by investing all that you have in whatever you do. Then others will come along side you to support what you are doing." This has been the key to our ministry over the past 20 years. Randa and I invested all that we had into the work of the Kingdom and then a few years later, many came along side and invested in this Kingdom work with us. Today, we proudly call it, **Transform Asia.** Your input into my life has been and will forever be appreciated.

Your last words of encouragement to your family in the Intensive Care Unit at the University Hospital in Aurora, Colorado, are unforgettable. You really demonstrated the great power and the meaningful, incredible love of Christ which you leave as a legacy to your kids, grand kids, great grandkids, friends, and caregivers. It is our prayer that your words keep reminding us to be faithful to Jesus and to one another. Dad, we are very proud of you for being so faithful to God, Mom, and all of us. We love you so much and you will forever be in our hearts, minds, and souls.

Your Son,

Setan Aaron Lee

ACKNOWLEDGEMENTS

꩜

Writing this book with Setan and Randa Lee has been an experience of a life time. The stories of their lives are both heart wrenching and filled with great joy and celebration. It is a privilege to know them and to see how they live out their great faith and trust in God day by day. There is one phrase that I hear over and over from both of them that will always stick with me. "Don't worry! God will provide." As they deal with all the things in their personal lives and in the lives of the multitude of people to whom they minister in Cambodia day by day, they truly believe that God will do everything He said He would. From the time I met them in the 1980's to now, they have been a wonderful example of love, faith, hope, and charity. I have loved working with them on this book.

The contributions of my wonderful friend, Della Musselman, to this book have been invaluable. She has worked on the Missions Committee, and as the Missions Secretary, at Faith Presbyterian Church for many years. Her very organized files on the work and lives of Setan and Randa Lee from the 1980's to the present are amazing. She willing opened them up for me to use in research for this book. She has also been my wonderful editor and advisor, and has worked with me from the first thought of doing this book. She has read and reread the manuscript as we made changes and additions over the long months of developing it. I have learned to love her red pencil markings, marginal notes and questions. Del, thank you from the depth of my heart. I love you and admire your great heart and willingness to work endless hours with us on this project. You are the best!

Jerry Simmons is another person I must acknowledge and thank for his remarkable help. He has been a long time friend, but has not been involved in the lives of the Lees until very recently. I asked him to read the first draft of the manuscript for this book and tell me if there were places in the story that were unclear or difficult to understand.

When we met to discuss this, he was filled with questions, and had marked places he felt more information would be good, or more emphasis. Jerry, thank you so much! Your questions and insight were a great help and also led to the addition of a little historical background on Cambodia.

There are several people who are part of my life and also have known the Lee family from the time they arrived in Colorado. Some of them were able to give me some insights in certain areas of the early part of the Lee's lives in the United States. They know who they are, and I thank each of you for your input as I was working on this book.

I believe that many people will be touched by the story of God's great work in the lives and ministries of Setan and Randa Lee. To God be the glory, praise, and honor for all He has and will accomplish with their lives, and in mine.

Shelba Hammond

TABLE OF CONTENTS

❦

FOREWARD

꧁꧂

"In this world you will have trouble. But take heart! I have overcome the world." John 16:33 (NIV)

The typical view of the Christian life is that it means to be delivered in adversity. You will run through a lot of emotions as read this story. You will be confronted with the crudity of man to do evil beyond your imagination. You will be astounded at the numerous first-hand miracles that "God of the Universe" has done. You will find hope in whatever situation you are going through, that if God did it for Setan, He can do it for you as well.

This book can introduce you to this God of the Universe, and take your life in a completely new direction, as He did for Setan.

We will see what can happen to one man who says yes to "God of the Universe" and the tens of thousands of lives that have been changed, and are being changed around the world.

You may want to be a supporter of this ministry; I have and have been blessed.

Warning: Once you start to read you may not be able to stop.

Evangelist William Fay
Author/Speaker: "Share Jesus
With Out Fear"

CAMBODIA
A Little Historical Background

❧

King Norodom of Cambodia was helpless to defend his country against its aggressive neighbors who had set out to divide his land among them. Being cognizant of his desperate situation, in 1864 he requested protection from the French government. It is doubtful the king realized the extent of change this would bring to his country and its future. Cambodia would remain under the wings of the French until 1953. During that time, Cambodia's kings became mere figureheads and the people saw them as god-kings. No longer did they rule their own country.

French exploitation of Cambodia's natural resources, plus much dissidence within the members of the royal family, took a huge toll on the country and its people. Poverty and suffering reigned for many years and Cambodia's Monarchy had no power to change the course of things.

In the 1880's, Cambodia was brought into the French-controlled Indochinese Union. This proved to be an extremely arduous and perplexing time for Cambodia. The people suffered through great discrimination by the Indochinese Union. Many of the peasants lost their farms due to high taxation and high interest rates. Revolts by the peasants were not uncommon, but little changed no matter what they did to make their plight known.

Much of the territory on the western side of Cambodia was traded to Thailand in the 1890's in exchange for their position of political control over much of Cambodia. This area remained under Thai rule for over a decade. However, through a border treaty, these territories were returned to Cambodia in 1907. The people of Cambodia had no say in these matters.

The French knew they couldn't do away with the royal family; that would create havoc in the country. But their control extended even to which member of the royal family would be king. However, the people had the ear of the kings, who could make it easier for the French leaders, or they could negatively influence the people's response toward them. Yet the people could only watch as King Norodom was replaced in 1904 by King Sisowath who was friendlier toward the French. He remained in power until 1927 when he was succeeded by King Sisowath Monivong. Then in 1941, the French installed Prince Norodom Sihanouk, the 19 year old great grandson of King Norodom. They felt that he would be more pliable in their hands. The French controlled the monarchy and politics, and it trickled down into almost every aspect of the people's lives.

The country came through World War II (1940-45), almost unscathed. During the Japanese occupation, the French continued to manage the affairs of Cambodia. When the war ended, they regained complete control of the country. Life continued to be difficult because the French did nothing to improve the daily lives of the people. Education was mostly neglected, and the extreme taxation and other mistreatment and suppression of the people continued to make life miserable. Prince Sihanouk became very aware of the people's cries. After several tumultuous years, he took some unexpected action. He led a crusade for independence from the French and the people were very united behind him. *The young Prince had matured and wasn't so pliable anymore!* Cambodia became an independent nation on November 9, 1953.

Independence brought much optimism. Cambodia began to flourish and day to day life was much better. Under the Prince's rule, the infrastructure of the country began to surge. They built better roads, beautiful homes and hospitals, as well as schools and universities to educate their young people.

A few problems began to surface in the 1960's during the war between North and South Vietnam due to the infiltration of Vietnamese people escaping into Cambodia. Many of the Cambodian peasants especially resented their jobs being taken by these people. The quality of life for many of the people began to disintegrate; especially the poorer people.

Then on March 18, 1970, the Lon Nol government (backed by the United States), easily deposed Prince Norodom Sihanouk, forcing him into exile in Beijing, China. However, much of the nation didn't seem to realize the impact this would have in the not too distant future.

The Cambodian public was totally unaware of a young man in their midst, Saloth Sar, who had been a student in Paris. While there he studied the Marxist ideals which he would later distort to support his own murderous regime. He was called by several names before he became the infamous Pol Pot that would later head the Khmer Rouge. But he would remain in the shadows until 1975.

The Khmer Rouge was home-based communists who were trying to overthrow the United States-backed Lon Nol government. They had earlier received support and training from the North Vietnamese soldiers who had hidden in the jungles of Cambodia. They became fully trained in guerilla warfare. In a few short years, this would be a ready army for Pol Pot and his scheme of a totalitarian regime.

PROLOGUE

SETAN LEE WAS THE SON OF CHAN Lee, a man who grew up in poverty, but had become a wealthy businessman in Cambodia. Chan had been very ambitious and was determined to be a very successful business man. Through years of long, hard work, he had built an import-export business that was extremely successful and prosperous. He reached a financial position that allowed him to give his family the best in all areas of life – a beautiful home, the best education, and great esteem in the community. Remembering his own back-ground, Mr. Lee taught his children to treat all people with dignity, regardless of their background or their current social standing. He and Mrs. Lee taught Setan and his siblings to share their good fortune with children who were less privileged. However, the future of their children was of utmost importance to them, so they made certain that all their children got the best education available, including private tutors when needed to help them advance.

Due to these privileges, Setan finished high school at the age of 14. He had wanted to be a doctor from the time he was a small child, so at age 15, he began attending medical school. He was extremely excited to be in the medical school, and almost had to pinch himself to believe he was actually there. He could envision his future. He would work hard and become the best doctor in Cambodia! He was the youngest student in his class, but he was as capable as any of the other students.

Monthy, Setan's older brother was studying to be a pharmacist. "It was our dream that I would have my own clinic and Monthy would have a pharmacy next to the clinic," Setan recalled. They made big plans for their future, but they kept in mind the things instilled in them by their parents. "It was our hope to get enough business from the wealthy that we could help the poor people as well," Setan stated.

However, in early 1975, due to military conflicts in the country, the medical school where Setan attended classes in Phnom Penh was frequently closed. Setan and Monthy became very concerned that their education might be interrupted, or even that they might not be able to complete their studies if the fighting continued to escalate. So the two brothers began to plan for a bold move; they would go to Paris to continue their education.

Monthy wanted to leave right away and get things set up for both of them, and begin his classes there as soon as possible. Setan would join him in June when he finished the school year. But, when their parents were told of their plans, they immediately stopped them because they felt that Setan (not yet 18 years old) was just too young to travel abroad alone. Monthy was not pleased with their decision, but they insisted that he was to wait until June and the brothers could travel to Paris together.

It would have been only a couple of months before Setan and Monthy would move to Paris. But in that brief time, something occurred that would change their plans forever.

~*~*~

It was the last day of the Cambodian New Year, April 17, 1975. Eighteen year-old Setan had picked up his best friend, Dara, in his new white truck and driven to Buddhist Temple Square in Battambang, the second largest city in Cambodia. The Cambodian New Year was always a time of great celebration. Like all the other young people who had gathered in the square that day, they planned to have a lot of fun and enjoy all the festivities. The people were bustling and noisy with music and laughter and congratulating each other in the New Year. Everyone was in a joyful and celebratory mood.

Almost unnoticed at first, huge trucks loaded with soldiers in black uniforms drove into the square. They began piling out of the trucks, aiming their guns at the people and shouting "Enemy! Enemy! Enemy!" The people in the square were terrified but had no idea what was happening.

Setan and Dara certainly didn't understand and were as frightened as everyone else. Why were the soldiers calling them enemies? Somehow, Dara found the courage to approach one of the soldiers to ask what was going on. Realizing these soldiers were also

Cambodians, he said to them, "I'm not your enemy! Why do you call me your enemy?"

The soldier's actions were quick and shocking. "Just like that, they shot Dara and killed him," Setan recalled. "I was numb with terror." He knew that Dara was already dead; there was nothing he could do for his friend. It crossed his mind to find a gun and try to fight back. But as the shooting continued the crowds began to scream and run, climbing over the walls to get away. Many things were tumbling through Setan's mind, but he didn't know what to do or where to go. He wanted to run, but he couldn't! He began to panic.

Suddenly, the shooting stopped. The soldiers still held their rifles on the people that had not gotten over the walls and began ordering them to put their hands over their heads. Trembling terribly, Setan lifted his hands high. He had no idea where he would be taken or what would happen to him. He remembered that several members of his family had planned to visit their relatives that day, so he began to pray that they would escape across the border into Thailand to safety. It didn't take long for him to realize that life as he knew it had come to an end. With his hands held high over his head, he was herded along with all the others at the point of the soldiers' guns. How had this happened?!

~*~*~

Prior to Pol Pot's arrival on the scene, the Khmer Rouge soldiers frequently attacked the Cambodian Army, and the army fought back again and again. Because of the invading Vietnamese, civil war became a way of life. Even though it caused great concern and frequent inconvenience, the Cambodian way of life had continued much as it had been for many years, especially for the upper-class citizens. Setan Lee and his family were no different than most of the other elite citizens of Cambodia during this time. They had not realized that the Khmer Rouge under the leadership of Pol Pot was poised to do whatever they deemed necessary to take over their country and force upon them a completely totalitarian regime. This would change their lives forever.

Chapter 1

IMPRISONMENT
April, 1975

૮ৡৡ৾৽

K HMER ROUGE SOLDIERS HELD
rifles on their captives in the Temple
Square and began shouting orders. Having
just seen his best friend shot to death, Setan
Lee immediately distrusted the soldiers completely. He was frozen in his tracks as he stood
there with his hands over his head along with
all the other people in the square. He was certain that something was terribly wrong; the
soldiers were not telling them where they
would be taken. He had understood for some
time that the Khmer Rouge considered the
wealthy and educated people of Cambodia
their enemies, but what was happening now
didn't make sense. His mind was spinning in

many directions, but it was clear to him that the city was being forcefully evacuated.

Then a soldier looked directly at Setan and ordered him to go home and change into his school uniform. He ran home, but he knew he would not put on his uniform. After all, these soldiers had just killed his best friend right in front of him. Why would he believe anything they said? If the soldiers saw his school uniform they would know he and his family were members of the elite citizens of Battambang, and he would be considered their enemy. Instead, Setan put on old, dirty clothing, hoping to keep his true identity from them. He wasn't sure what he should do. He knew if he didn't come out, they would come looking for him. So he ran out into the street, joining the terrified crowds who were being marched out of the city at gun point.

As the throngs of people moved along, one of the soldiers stopped Setan in the middle of the street and asked how long he'd had his shoes. Setan told him that he'd had them maybe a couple of months. The soldier ordered him to remove his shoes and give them to him. Setan complied with the order. Walking barefoot, Setan's feet were soon cut, bruised and bleeding. He was in a lot of pain as they traveled the remainder of the day over rough and rocky roads. Even the pain and uncertainty did not stop the turmoil in Setan's head.

The next day, well outside the city, they came upon a shocking site as they approached some rice fields. He saw professors, teachers, students in uniforms, and Cambodian military officers, among other professional people being taken from long lines of vehicles. The soldiers marched them into the rice fields and began shooting them. Some of the soldiers made them kneel down before they killed them. Many were shot in the back of the head where they stood. Setan was horrified as he watched. The rice fields were filled with bloody bodies!

Setan soon realized that the vehicles were unloading and returning to the city to bring more victims to the fields. Suddenly, Setan recognized his father's new car. He began praying that his father was not in the car. Then he saw a general, one of his father's best friends, get out of the car. He was smiling and waving his hands, shouting, "Victory! Victory!" But as the general celebrated, he was shot in the back of the head and killed. Setan saw that as the passengers unloaded

Pol Pot's last stronghold in Anlong Veng

from the car, each one was killed. He felt paralyzed as the horror played out before him.

Then, he saw his father get out of the car, and a soldier had a rifle pointed at his head. Setan started to scream, "No! No!" Without thought of the soldiers all around him, he began running toward his father. He didn't care that he might be killed. He just ran.

Setan had no way of knowing that those soldiers were only keeping control of the situation. He could not have known that his father was being forced at gunpoint to drive people to these rice fields to their death. For the moment, his father was useful to the soldiers.

His father was shocked to see him, but he embraced Setan and began begging the soldiers to let him have a moment with his son. Amazingly, they allowed them to talk, but kept guns pointed at them as they shouted, "Quickly! Quickly!" Setan asked his father why he was there and why he had not gone into Thailand since the border was so close. His father replied that the family had been waiting for him, that they could not think of leaving without him.

Setan was so stricken with grief and guilt. He realized that his entire family had been captured because they were waiting for him. As they took his father away, Setan was ushered back into the crowd being forced out of the city.

~*~*~

There were three rules in a Khmer Rouge concentration camp: Don't ask questions; don't show any emotions; do either and you will die. Setan Lee was constantly on edge, afraid of what would happen next. He saw friends tortured – fingernails pulled out, tongues cut out – and watched helplessly as others died all around him. He was continually on guard, trying to stay alert to the orders of his captors.

Although the guards at the camp were very suspicious of his pretended illiteracy, seventeen year-old Setan was placed in a youth concentration camp for illiterates. This camp was located in Veal Prarm Roy (meaning 500 fields) near the Cambodian border. Setan knew he must continue to portray himself as an uneducated farm boy for his own survival. He knew he had to carry out this incredible acting job since his skin was much too light to have worked on a farm, and his hands were not calloused from manual labor. So, he was ordered to work in the fields for long hours every day.

God had blessed Setan with a photographic memory which enabled him to quickly pick up on the proper use of an axe and other farm tools. He had to catch on fast or it would be his life! He had to learn very quickly how to plow and do other farm chores that the other young people seemed to know instinctively how to accomplish. However, his farming prowess did not convince his captors completely, so he was soon moved to another youth concentration camp.

Conditions at the new camp were even more deplorable. The young prisoners were forced to work from 4 a.m. to midnight, twenty hours a day. They did this on a starvation diet of liquid rice soup which included a few bad vegetables, but with no salt. The human body must have salt to prevent it from breaking down completely, and becoming bloated and swollen. So, many inmates resembled walking balloons with huge swollen chins and stomachs. Many were walking zombies and soon died even as they strived to survive. Death came due to starvation, malaria, dysentery, and pneumonia.

Frequently, Setan would wake up in the middle of the night with his body submerged in water, and had to sit up to keep from drowning. He would think to himself, "If I can just live through this hour, I'll be lucky." His bed was mud and his ceiling was the sky. Guards, some younger than Setan, would beat him just for the fun of it and laugh about it. Once they even held a candle to Setan's arm and a piece of burning wood to the other arm until the flesh began to fall off – just for their own amusement. The physical torture was terrible, but the emotional torture was burned into him even more deeply.

For a brief time, Setan and some members of his family were assigned to work on the same irrigation system. They had all managed to keep their identities hidden from their captors. It was a difficult time because any encounter with a family member had to be quick, and any conversation very brief. It was the only way they would survive. They could not risk being caught talking to each other. Each day their nerves were on edge for fear of their guards catching on to their true situation. This difficult reunion was much too short and very heart wrenching when they had to part again.

There was another short period of time when the prisoners were crowded into an abandoned temple. They weren't sure what to expect, but soon the guards picked Setan out of the group and forced him to smash a statue of the Buddha. Setan was the grandson of a Buddhist priest whom he loved deeply, and who had taught him the Buddhist religion. He was very upset, but he had no choice but to do as he was told. "I could not sleep," he said. "I thought I had killed my god and he would take revenge on me."

Being very religious, Setan was extremely frightened as he waited for his god's revenge. But nothing happened. Setan's grandfather had taught him that there was a higher power and this god was more powerful than anything else on earth. Yet, as time passed and no revenge came, Setan's faith in his god began to fade. "There was no power or force to support belief in my god anymore," Setan said. "I knew there had to be something out there, and if not Buddha, who could it be?" But the struggle to survive took all the strength Setan had, so he soon quit pondering this question.

As the days passed he felt more and more hopeless. The little amounts of scalding rice soup they were given had to be gulped down quickly and then back to work. The lack of nutrition soon destroyed the prisoner's gums and teeth. Most of the time, Setan just hoped he could make it through the next hour. He watched his friends as they died of untreated malaria, dysentery, pneumonia or starvation. This was a nightmare existence.

The prisoners would eat anything they could get their hands on to supplement their less than meager diets, even though having their own food was strictly forbidden. They would gulp down whole frogs, fish, crabs, and insects they found in the swampy work fields. If they were caught eating these things, it could mean instant death at the hands of their guards.

One day, a young friend found a crab and passed it to Setan. She thought she had not been seen, but a young female guard was watching. The girl was sentenced to die on the spot. Setan begged and protested for his friend's life, but to no avail. The young guard placed a plastic bag over her head and the girl suffocated in a few short minutes. To Setan, it seemed like forever as she gasped for air and for her life while their amused captors watched and laughed. Setan screamed in sheer terror as he witnessed his friend's ghastly death.

Then, it was Setan's turn. He was terrified! But instead of killing him, the guards dragged him to some nearby railroad tracks. There they buried him in a deep hole with dirt and rocks covering his entire body. Only his head was exposed. In this place that was plentiful with poisonous snakes and wild animals, they left him to die.

However, a higher power had other plans for Setan Lee. After two long and anguishing days and nights, two Khmer Rouge female soldiers came upon him and had mercy on him. They pulled him from his intended grave, but they did not return him to his previous camp. Instead, they took him to their own camp. Setan could not walk; his legs were paralyzed. So his captors placed him in a little hut at the foot of Phnom Toch, which means 'Small Mountain.' It was here the Khmer Rouge leaders grew their gardens, and where they could come and relax for days at a time.

Setan could do nothing but sit in this little hut and roll to a nearby area which he used for "bathroom" needs. Working for them seemed impossible in his condition. But the ladies found a way to make him useful. They would bring water and firewood to where Setan was sitting and he had to build a fire and boil the water for them. This was about all he was really able to do in the way of work. So, the ladies asked that he sing patriotic songs for their amusement. Setan said, "I knew I had to please them, so I sang with a big fake smile and gusto to make them happy with my efforts."

After eight months the paralysis slowly subsided and he was able to walk again. The guards then returned him to his previous camp in the "killing fields" where he was treated even more harshly than before. He had to watch as friends had their eyes gouged out, acid poured on their faces, and plastic held over their heads long enough to cause paralysis, but not death. Some were able to endure this, but others could not. Many would slit their own throats at night to relieve the agony.

"Countless times I considered ending it all by committing suicide as many of my friends had done" Setan stated. "However, something in me told me to keep going – I would make it through all of this."

Just as he convinced himself that he could make it, the unthinkable happened. His student ID card which he had hidden in a small pocket in his pants was found! The ID card told his captors that he was a member of the educated class, a city dweller, and an arch enemy of the Khmer Rouge. He was immediately sentenced to die along with four other students.

They were bound, blindfolded, and led to an open field. Setan stood helplessly and heard the cries of his friends as they were hacked to death with a bamboo branch that had no leaves, just deadly sharp barbs. He felt the spatter of the warm blood of his friends on his face as each one died an agonizing death. He was the only one left – now it was his turn to die. Setan began to cry out, "Lord of the Universe, whoever you are, please spare my life!"

Where had those words come from? Never in his Buddhist upbringing had he ever prayed a prayer like that. His executioners shoved him to his knees and he felt the bamboo branch that had killed his friends close to his neck, ready to fall and send him to his death. Setan felt sure this was his end. There was no escape.

Chapter 2

"THE LORD OF THE UNIVERSE"

ᗕᗒᗓᗔ

A S SETAN LEE WAITED FOR THE deadly blow, a loud voice screamed from behind him. "STOP! We must investigate this man further!" What?! There was no such thing as investigations in the killing fields. And, there was never an investigation prior to an execution! Setan's mind was racing with these thoughts, not having any idea what would happen next.

The blindfold was yanked from his eyes and they immediately fell on the ghastly scene of the mutilated bodies of his fellow students. He instantly knew that whomever or whatever he had screamed out to just moments before had spared his life. He knew in his heart that he had just left his Buddhist upbringing to now serve this new found faith – whatever it was.

Setan was taken to a small building nearby that was a station for the Khmer Rouge leaders. Although he didn't realize it at the time, the very education that had led to his capture and torture was now going to be the very instrument that would save his life. He was quickly seated at a small table and was handed a piece of paper and a pencil. His captors then gave him what seemed to be an insurmountable task.

Despite the boasting of the Khmer Rouge that the country was progressing and moving rapidly ahead, its rice production was going down considerably. The government needed drastic measures in order to feed a much maligned and starving nation. So, they ordered Setan to design an irrigation system to bolster the faltering rice production. He was educated, so they surmised he could do this!

But, Setan had been a medical student with no training whatsoever in agriculture or engineering. He thought to himself, "They may as well have gone ahead and killed me because I have no earthly idea how to design an irrigation system for rice or anything else." He was about to confess his ignorance and seal his fate of death yet another time. But instead, he found himself placing the pencil on the paper and beginning to draw. Setan said later, "Something inside me forced me to sketch out a design for an irrigation system to bring water from a river I had never even seen." Where it came from or from whom, he did not know. It was a drawing that miraculously saved his life again! He handed the paper to the Khmer Rouge leader. It was examined, and amazingly, it was declared perfect.

Even more amazing, this irrigation system was very quickly put into production! The irrigation system drawn by Setan Lee, a medical student, not an engineer, is still being used to this very day!

The next day, the guard who had killed Setan's friend for giving him the crab called him to her house. "I called you here because I want to ask you to marry me," she said.

Setan now understood why she had suffocated his friend. She was in love with him and thought his friend might be a rival female. She was so jealous of his friend that she killed her in a fit of rage. He knew his next words must be carefully chosen or they might be his very last.

"Please allow me to become more mature in the revolution first; then I will marry you," Setan graciously explained. Inside he laughed at the words he had just spoken, knowing he would rather die than marry this demented woman.

"Okay, you can mature yourself in the revolution first, and then we will be married," the befuddled woman retorted. She was not happy with his request, but she allowed Setan to return to his post.

As the months passed during 1978, Setan heard almost constant gunfire in the distance and it came closer and closer to his location day by day. At the outset of the Khmer Rouge takeover, North Vietnam had been its staunchest ally. Now the Cambodian Liberation Forces, with the support of the North Vietnamese were capturing Cambodian land more and more each passing day.

Setan knew nothing about the politics going on around him, but as the gunfire moved closer to him, he knew this could prove to be his best opportunity for escape. Confusion in his midst might provide a way to escape unnoticed. But he knew that he had to choose the right time.

His opportunity came a few days later. As the invading Cambodian Liberation Forces and North Vietnamese came closer, the guards ordered the prisoners to run into the woods to avoid capture. Setan knew this was his time and he had better think fast – and think fast he did! He didn't run with the prisoners, but instead hid himself in an irrigation ditch face down. He could hear the Khmer Rouge soldiers calling his name. But as the gunfire came closer, the soldiers themselves ran into the jungle to avoid capture. Setan didn't move! After several hours, he slowly rose from the ditch and ran alone into the jungle.

He knew his only route of escape was to head west to Thailand with hope of crossing the border as quickly as possible. Between him and the border were deadly mine fields that were strewn with body after mangled body. These corpses proved to be his map for navigating the mine fields. As he stepped on each body, most were already dead, but he realized that some were still alive. Knowing there was nothing he could do to help any of them, he continued using each as a stepping stone to freedom.

Setan spent several nights in this strange and eerie jungle. He ate whatever leaves and fruit he could find and drank water from the hollows of trees or from ditches cluttered with dead bodies. When he heard soldiers approaching, he would lie still for hours. When he felt it was safe again, he would then move farther west toward Thailand.

During his journey toward freedom, something very strange happened. As Setan was standing alone in the jungle, a man suddenly grabbed his arm. The man was dressed very poorly and seemed to be barely alive. Setan gained his composure after being scared half to death. The man mumbled something that echoed peculiarly in Setan's ears. "Do you believe in the Lord of the universe?" he asked Setan. Setan was too stunned to answer. "Do you believe in the Lord of the universe?" the man repeated.

As Setan searched his mind as to why these words rang so clearly, he quickly remembered what he had prayed earlier just before being spared from execution. He had prayed to *"the Lord of the Universe"* to be spared from death. The man kept repeating, "Do you believe in the Lord of the universe?"

Setan looked into his eyes and exclaimed, "Yes. I do believe in the Lord of the universe."

"His name is Jesus Christ," the man said to Setan. "Would you like to accept Jesus as your Savior and Lord? He will give you eternal life. You and I may not have much time. Any minute now, either of us could step on a land mine and die!"

Setan answered, "Yes, I accept Jesus as my Savior!" Then almost as quickly as he had appeared, the tattered prophet disappeared into the jungle as gunfire flew over their heads.

"I sincerely believe that man was a messenger from God," Setan later explained. "I had never heard of Christianity, but that day I became a Christian. That was the moment of my conversion to Christianity."

After more than a month in the jungle, Setan was running toward the Thailand border. Along the way, the bullets were still flying around him. At times, he fell to the ground, crawling on his stomach. When he could run, he was constantly dodging behind trees or whatever he could to avoid the bullets. The enemy's pursuit seemed endless. Setan was so exhausted physically and mentally, he could hardly stay on his feet. He feared he would be captured again. Just when he thought he might not make it, he suddenly saw a man in a spotless white uniform waving a big Red Cross flag and standing with his arms outstretched, indicating that Setan was about to cross the Cambodian-Thailand border.

"It was just like heaven seeing this man in his spotless white uniform reach out to me," Setan exclaimed. "I was so dirty and smelled so bad, I ran right past this very clean man. I was so embarrassed. I didn't want to get him all dirty and I knew that I had to stink. After all, I had not had a real bath in nearly four years. Even so, I was so excited and began running all around behind where the man was standing, crying with joy. Suddenly, this man in his white uniform embraced me from behind! I felt safe, loved, and secure in the strong arms of this man. It was like being in a dream."

Setan could hardly believe that he had truly escaped from his horrible Khmer Rouge captors! The man from the Red Cross took him into a refugee camp in Thailand where thousands of other refugees had been taken in. Setan knew he would have food to eat and a place to clean himself and his clothing. ***The***

Lord of the Universe had led him to a place of safety.

Today, as Setan thinks back on this exciting day, it reminds him of a story in the Bible, in Mark 1: 40-44, where the leper came to Jesus for cleansing. In those days, the lepers were pushed outside the cities because their skin and flesh was so destroyed by the leprosy that they were considered unworthy of living among other people. They were considered 'unclean.' If anyone came close to them, they had to loudly shout, "Unclean! Unclean!" Then the people would quickly go away from them and leave them in their place of pain and struggle.

But when the leper in Mark chapter one came to Jesus, he said to the Lord, "If You are willing, You can make me clean."

Then Jesus, moved with compassion, stretched out His hand and touched the leper and said to him, "I am willing; be cleansed." The leprosy immediately left him and he was clean.

That is what Jesus does for us when we come to Him. He cleanses us from all our sins and the filthy things in our lives. He gives us a life of safety, and a life free of all those dirty, smelly things that were previously in our lives. He forgives us completely and makes us clean and whole. No matter where He leads us, we are safe and loved, and secure in His arms!

Setan explained, "As I crossed into Thailand, that is how I felt as I stood in the arms of this man in a white uniform! I was safe and secure; I knew I would have a clean place to stay with food and shelter, unlike the life I'd had in the killing fields of Cambodia."

A few days after Setan was taken to the Thailand Refugee Camp, he and a number of other refugees were trucked down to Khoa I Dang, another refugee camp. It didn't matter where the Red Cross took him or sent him; he was safe and that was all that mattered.

Chapter 3

SUDDEN END OF CHILDHOOD

✋

O N THAT FATEFUL DAY IN APRIL of 1975, Randa Yos was spending a relaxing holiday with her family at their home in Battambang. Her father was the president of the local university and had gone to his office that morning. Even though they were a Buddhist family, they did not plan on celebrating the New Year.

Randa's mother and father divorced when she was pre-school age and she and all but one of her siblings lived in her father's home. However, her father's job required frequent travel, so Randa was brought up by her aunt and grandmother until he remarried when she was nine years old. Randa knew that her mother and her youngest sister lived a short distance outside the city, but she couldn't understand why she wasn't allowed to visit them. She was frequently troubled about this, sometimes feeling depressed and unhappy.

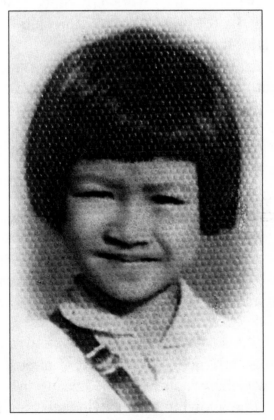

Randa Yos (grade school)

Her father and his second wife soon had two other children. With her father's busy schedule, which frequently took him away from home for days at a time, and the growing family the house was always filled with activity. Randa remembers those hectic days and how she missed her father when he was away. But, they were a privileged family and had a lot more than most people in the country. It was a good life.

Randa's father frequently reminisced about the difficult days of World War II, and explained to his children that if war came to Cambodia they might have much less to eat, and many things might be more difficult. This didn't faze Randa. She was just too young to grasp the realities of her father's words. She had always been a finicky eater, and still refused to eat fish with bones, vegetables and meats with fat. She cried if she was asked to finish her food. She felt safe in his love and care and had no real concept of the concerns he was expressing to his family.

All this was far from Randa's mind on this holiday afternoon. At the age of almost 13, she was enjoying a fun time because her sisters were allowing her to style their hair, one of her favorite things to do. Even though they had become somewhat accustomed to the riots and gunfire that sometimes even caused them to miss school, she was too young to understand it. None of them were prepared for the interruption that would end their fun-filled day.

Suddenly gunfire and shouting erupted outside. Randa's cousin burst into the room screaming that Randa's father had just been taken by the Khmer Rouge. Then they all heard a loud speaker shouting out instructions that all residents were to prepare to go to an unknown destination. They were told to leave everything behind and leave their homes immediately because Americans were on their way to bomb Battambang.

Randa's family was frightened beyond words as they quickly departed their home. They moved toward the village outside of Battambang where their father had grown up. They hoped their father would look there for them since they had no idea which direction he had been taken.

Meanwhile, the Khmer Rouge soldiers had burst into Mr. Yos' office at the university. He was among hundreds of people loaded into vehicles and taken away. He was taken to a place he did not recognize, having no idea what was happening. Suddenly, he saw a man he had worked with in earlier years who he knew to be a Communist. The man warned him that he had to escape from the Khmer Rouge and try to find his family. "They plan to kill all of you," the man said. He knew exactly what was happening and helped Randa's father to escape.

Randa and her family continued toward their destination the next morning. They were walking on the narrow, crowded road that ran beside the river when Randa saw her father riding a bicycle, calling out his family's names! They were all greatly relieved to have the family together again and continued to make their way toward her father's village. They talked about all that had happened to them the day before.

They later learned that most of Randa's family was not as fortunate as they had been. The day of the attacks, the Khmer Rouge had killed all of her father's extended family, even the babies.

However, the relief Randa's family had felt at being reunited was short lived. Three weeks later all families were split apart and sent to different concentration camps around the country. Young children were separated from their parents and sent to different camps to work in the rice fields and farms.

Randa was sent to a children's camp for thirteen to sixteen year olds. There, she labored for 20 hours daily working in rice fields and carrying rocks and dirt for an irrigation ditch. She slept where she worked – in the field, resting as best she could on the dirt and rocks.

"If you were lucky, you might get to sleep under a tree that might protect you from the rain," Randa explained, " but most of the time you just got wet, and learned to sleep whenever and wherever you got the chance."

The food wasn't much better than the sleeping arrangement. Thin rice soup with a few vegetables thrown in was the usual diet. "About what you would feed a pig," Randa explained.

Many times when the prisoners were supposed to be getting much needed sleep, they were forced to listen to indoctrination speeches. Randa was often so tired she would fall asleep but would almost always wake up just in time to clap with the others for the ridiculous dialogue. "They told us to be loyal to the party, to be brave," she said. "None of us believed a word of it and would just try to get through it without falling asleep."

Thus, the weeks and months passed as Randa remained in this children's camp. Little changed as the days went by – just more hard work and terrible food.

Before the New Year in 1976, a day came when her hopes of seeing her family were bolstered. Thousands of workers had been sent to build a dam nearby. There in the midst of a sea of men and women, Randa spotted her father. "He was so very, very skinny," Randa said. She couldn't risk talking to him, but as quickly as she could, she inquired about the workers. She seemed to have found favor with one of her captors, and she told Randa a little about the camp these men were assigned to.

In the middle of the night Randa sneaked out of the camp and traveled the few miles to her father's camp and found him. He was so happy to see her! They cried and cried as they reminisced about the family and shuddered as they thought of the menacing and uncertain future. It was wonderful just to see her father again. Soon Randa had to leave and sneak back into her camp.

There were several different children's camps located not too far from each other.

When they were taken out on work assignments, sometimes the children in one camp would be working in the same area as another children's camp. A few days after Randa had found her father and talked with him, she saw one of her sisters from another camp working nearby. She was able to get close enough to her sister to learn which camp she was assigned to. They quickly made a plan to meet.

Later that night, they met and traveled the short distance to their father's camp so they could spend some time with him. They decided they would do this as often as possible. They were very concerned about their father's health; he was so frail. In later visits, they took food they had saved during the day to give to their father, even though he always refused it, telling them they needed it more than him.

It is almost unbelievable that the sisters were able to come and go as many times as they did to meet at their father's camp with him. Why didn't the guards at his camp see them? Was Someone watching over all of them all those times?

During this time, their father learned that his wife was sick in a nearby camp and knew that she was burdened with taking care of their two toddlers. He took a very great risk and asked if he could visit her. He was told he could, but only after he had personally built a dike some 500 yards over a rice paddy.

After learning about this, each evening Randa and her sister would sneak out of their camps and work most of the night helping their father finish the dike more quickly. At times, it seemed the dike would never be finished. But finally the day came when it was finished and their father prepared to leave to visit his wife and small children. Early the next morning, Randa's father left to visit his wife.

That evening, Randa heard horses galloping through her camp and wondered what was going on. Because Randa had made a habit of helping the leaders in the camp with many chores, she was in their tent that evening. As she worked she overheard them talking about gathering people who would be taken away. She asked one of the leaders what all the commotion was about. What the woman told her chilled her to the bone. They were gathering up all doctors, lawyers and professional people – all those who hadn't been already taken away. Randa sheepishly asked the woman if she could look at the list of the condemned. She quickly spotted her father's name and the words "taken away" written next to his name. "What that meant was he was never coming back," Randa recalled. "It meant they would kill him." She wanted to cry. Tears welled up inside her, but she couldn't allow them to come or she would be killed for showing emotion for an enemy of the state.

Meanwhile, the soldiers in her father's camp knew that he had left earlier in the day to go to his wife's camp in the nearby village. So they followed him and captured him before he could reach his family.

Randa wasn't aware of this. She waited and watched; her mind was in turmoil. She knew that her father had gone toward the village to look for his wife. If only she could get to that village. "What if – why not ask," she thought. She approached one of the leaders and timidly asked if she could go into the village to visit her relatives. The leader quickly refused her request. But Randa wasn't giving up – not yet.

She waited for darkness to fall and sneaked away, running as fast as she could. She hoped she could reach her father. If she could just get there in time! She ran in the pitch black darkness, falling many times, frequently into the river. Picking herself up again and again, she continued running as fast as her legs would carry her toward the village.

Things had really changed for Randa now. Not only had she become an enemy of the state for leaving the camp, but the Khmer Rouge now knew she was the daughter of a university president and a member of the elite class of Cambodia. If caught, her fate was sealed – death!

Randa reached the village just in time to see her father tied to the back of a horse, and being dragged behind it. She could do nothing but watch. She began screaming, but people around her urged her to stop screaming because they would kill her right there as well. The horse and rider pulling her father behind them disappeared in the distance and she never saw him again.

Randa could not stay in the village because everyone knew she belonged in the camp. So she returned, knowing she was in great trouble. When she arrived at her camp, they asked why she left without permission. She had no answer. The leaders of the camp could not help her now, even though one of them tried. Randa was told she would be taken to another camp because she was now condemned to die. She was quickly moved. "This was the camp where they send you to kill you. But before they kill you," Randa explained, "they made you work harder and harder for a long time, until you weaken to the point you can no longer function."

She now was given only one meager meal each day while she worked in rice paddies in water up to her thighs, or at times even up to her chest. During the rainy season, being so small, she had to tread water many times to keep from drowning. Plus, she had to deal with leaches. The big ones were easy to find and pull off, but the little ones clambered up her tiny legs and were ever so hard to locate and pull off. The filthy water caused her to develop raw blisters that covered her body from her waist to her toes. She was in constant pain and was sick most of the time with diarrhea and a fever so intense that she would frequently become unconscious. Scores of people passed out in the "killing fields," and most never regained consciousness to return to the grotesque working and living conditions. They were left there and their remains were eaten by wild animals and birds feasting on their flesh.

Randa was kept in this camp for many months. Her young eyes witnessed many atrocities in that camp – fingernails pulled out, guards forcing snakes on people that would inflict poisonous bites, and unmerciful deadly beatings. Some were tied to a tree and each day guards would return and cut the tiny slit in their throats a little larger until the prisoner bled to death. "They would never kill a person right away," Randa recalled, "but slowly so you would die suffering, not peacefully."

Amazingly, all these acts of violence didn't deter Randa; instead it fueled her resolve to live for the day she would escape from her villainous captors. She prayed for someone to come and be her hero and whisk her away from all this suffering and dying. "No matter what," she said, "I was not going to die young."

Randa worked in the fields day after day, never giving her captors any trouble. However, one morning she feigned sickness because she wanted to stay in the camp. She knew the rules – if she didn't work, she would not be given any food that day. But Randa was determined to stay there that day to see what goes on during the day. All the other workers and most of the leaders left the camp early, leaving Randa and a few other sick people behind.

About mid-morning, a convoy of military trucks came to a stop in the middle of Randa's camp. She watched as the trucks were being unloaded. When they finished unloading, the soldiers went inside for a short time. Randa seized her chance. She jumped into the back of one of the trucks and hid behind the seat closest to the cab of the truck. A canvas divider blocked the view of the soldiers in the front of the truck so that they could not see into the back of the truck. They pulled out the camp without knowing Randa was in the back of the truck. Though she guesses she was about fifteen years old at the time, she was still a very tiny young lady and fit easily into the small hiding place.

Later that day, the truck stopped to pick up two female soldiers who climbed into the back of the truck where Randa was hiding. As the trucks drove off again toward the jungle, one of the female soldiers heard a noise behind her seat, the seat Randa was hiding behind. Suddenly Randa's eyes met the soldier's eyes and both held their breath in complete shock.

Chapter 4

UNEXPECTED FRIENDSHIP

❧

RANDA WAS FROZEN WITH FEAR. She expected instant death – instead, the female soldier that had spotted her in the tiny hiding place casually moved closer to the cab of the truck, helping to further cover Randa. She shielded Randa from being seen by the other soldiers as the truck continued on through the military base. Randa was very scared, but knew she had to stay very still and not make a sound.

The truck soon arrived at another military base in the jungle and the driver jumped out. As soon as the soldier who was shielding Randa saw that no other soldiers were in sight, she ordered Randa from her hiding place onto the ground beside her. Randa immediately began to plead for her life.

Her captor ordered her to keep silent. She explained that she would spare Randa's life if she would agree to do all she told her to do. Randa was so happy the soldier wasn't going to kill her, she immediately agreed to do so. Whatever she had to do, her life was spared again.

She was taken to the female soldier's tent. There she was given a uniform and the woman informed Randa that she would be required to do the cooking, wash all the dishes, and whatever else she was asked to do. The woman reported to the other soldiers that the young girl would be staying with her to cook for her and keep her tent clean. Randa was safe for the time being.

She washed the soldier's clothes, cooked, and kept her tent clean and brought water for her baths. Randa did anything she was told to do – except for one thing. The soldier wanted to teach Randa how to shoot a rifle. Randa kept busy and shied away from this training because she did not even like to kill fish for food. She definitely had no intention of killing any person. Thankfully the soldier did not insist.

Randa soon became friends with her captor and was treated with some dignity by her. She learned that the soldier was the daughter of a school teacher and had been forced by the Khmer Rouge to join the military or be killed.

The military camp of her captor moved frequently to stay ahead of the oncoming North Vietnamese army. Randa remained in the soldier's camps for many months. Then early one morning Randa awoke to find her camp completely empty! All the soldiers had crept away into the jungle during the night. Her captor had left her there to face whatever the enemy would do.

She could hear the gunfire and exploding mines nearby, and she knew she had to get out! She quickly made the decision to escape across the border into Thailand. Randa knew the area because her captor had taken her along many times when she patrolled the border. She just didn't remember how far it was to the border or how long it would take her to get there. However, she was determined to make her way to what she hoped would be her long awaited freedom.

As she began the journey, she encountered corpses, wounded soldiers and dying countrymen. Fortunately she received some help along the way from fellow escapees and people in villages along the way who provided food and sometimes shelter. Life was difficult and full of dangers as she continued her journey toward Thailand.

As she wandered into an abandoned house to rest one day, she made a wonderful discovery. As soon as her eyes adjusted from the bright sunlight, she saw her sister and brother, an uncle and a cousin had also made their way to that same house! What a wonderful time they had as they all tried to talk at the same time in their big group hug. They too had been in concentration camps, but had escaped from their captors. They had decided they would try to return to the village where Randa's family had lived in Battambang. Now they began to tell Randa that she, too, should return to Battambang with them. She really wanted to continue on to Thailand, but relinquished this desire in order to stay with her family. She went back with them and found that her mother had also returned home to Battambang! It was a time of joyful reunion with her loved ones.

The North Vietnamese soldiers had taken control of her village and Randa had heard that these soldiers were all communists. She did not trust them at all. After a few weeks she decided that she must leave and try to get on to Thailand. She felt that they were not safe in Cambodia. She vowed she would return for her family. Her brother and sister begged to join Randa on this journey, but she convinced them it was too dangerous. Even though she was still a young teenager, she felt her chances of getting into Thailand were better if she went alone. She assured them she would return for them as soon as she could.

So Randa was off again to find freedom in Thailand. She traveled to a camp of Cambodian freedom fighters where people had to pay to get into the camp. Randa had no money. As she watched the people going into the camp, she hid herself among a large group of them and was granted entrance along with them. She quickly learned that the camp was not the safest place to be; she had to hide during the nights to escape being kidnapped or raped. She left there as soon as she could and continued on toward the border.

Randa still had no food and no means of getting it. Again, total strangers came to her aid. Two young women (who Randa later learned were Setan Lee's sisters) had mercy on her and invited her into their tent to eat with their family. Randa was very resourceful, so she built a small hut nearby and remained close to them. She helped the other family members gather food, water, and other necessities. Randa knew she was very fortunate to have these friends.

Soon, Randa, the Lee family (which did not include Setan), and others who were with them, all agreed that they must escape and get across the border into Thailand. So after dark that night, they made a run for it.

They ran like they had never run before with bullets flying inches over their heads from the North Vietnamese and the Cambodian freedom fighters. When the gunfire finally subsided, they hoped they might be safe. However, they didn't dare move a muscle. They remained very still the rest of the night, hoping the soldiers would not discover them.

Then daylight brought a wonderful sight! In the distance were people in the beautiful white uniforms of the Red Cross and the United Nations workers. They had made it! They ran into the waiting arms of these wonderful people, thankful beyond words to know they were finally in Thailand. They were safe at last.

In a very short time, they were loaded onto trucks and transported to the Khao I Dang refugee camp. Four years had passed since the journey began, and Randa was parted from her home and family. Randa Yos was now almost 17 years old and her persistence had paid off. She was now free! But her thoughts were still on her family in Battambang.

Chapter 5

CAMP KHAO I DANG

❧

THE FIRST MORNING AT THE refugee camp almost seemed like heaven to Setan Lee. For the first time in four torturous years, he was given a bar of soap. That kind of soap was probably meant to be used for cleaning clothes, but to Setan, it was beautiful. "That tiny bar of soap smelled so good, I wanted to eat it," Setan explained. "It was so precious and for the first time in four years, I got myself cleaned up!"

Then he feasted on the rice, fish and eggs that were provided for him. He was even allowed to cook his own eggs; he almost thought he had died and gone to heaven.

The camp at Khao I Dang was a picture of sorrow, poverty and hope all rolled together.

The fragrance of cooking fish and rice was abundant. There were daily scenes of families being rejoined for the first time in years. Then there was much evidence of pain on the faces of people learning that their loved ones had died or had been killed, never to be seen again. And, there were also faces of hope for a new beginning which many Cambodians had feared would never become reality.

Khoa I Dang housed more than 160,000 refugees by early 1980. It was a special camp because it was one of a few whose residents were eligible for resettlement outside the countries of Thailand or Cambodia.

During the following days and months of Setan's time in this camp, he was miraculously rejoined with several members of his family. They trickled in one, two, or even three at a time until several of them were accounted for. What joy and jubilation Setan and his family felt. Yet, what sorrow and guilt Setan experienced upon learning that his brother, Monthy, would not be returning.

Setan and Monthy had spent many hours dreaming of opening a clinic and pharmacy when they were both finished with their medical studies. Monthy could have gone to Paris to finish his studies, but instead, at his parent's insistence, stayed with Setan to support him in his studies. Setan learned that Monthy was captured and stood up to these Communist captors only to be shot to death in front of his friends.

The Killing Fields had taken a great toll on the Lee family. In Setan's extended family there were more than 38 who had been killed during the past four years. However, they would continue on with their new life, inspired by remembering the passing of many of their family members. There was so much to mourn and yet so much to celebrate. Setan still had his parents, his five sisters and his three younger brothers. And, there was someone else that would later bring him joy for the rest of his life. His family had adopted a very beautiful 17 year-old woman into their care – Randa Yos.

"She was so beautiful," Setan expressed. "I fell in love with her at first sight and knew then that I wanted to spend the rest of my life with her." For Randa, the feeling was not mutual.

Randa is holding the flowers (Age 16).

Setan met several Christian missionaries in the camp and began to spend much time with them discussing his new found faith. "It was during this time I realized that the One who saved me from being killed on several occasions, the One who gave me the knowledge to design the irrigation system, the One who brought my family back together – it was Jesus Christ!" Setan joyously explained.

One day as Setan was strolling through the camp, he came upon a man that looked very familiar. As he stared intently into the man's eyes, he realized it was the same man who had appeared to him in the jungle and had urged Setan to pray to the "Lord of the universe." This man ultimately became Setan's pastor and sought his help in building a new church in the refugee camp.

Setan was so excited about his new found faith and could not wait to awaken each morning to learn more about the Living God and his faith. Each day his pastor would teach him a new Scripture even though he had no Bible. He recited each verse to Setan from memory. Setan would diligently and meticulously memorize each word that came from his mentor's mouth. Then every afternoon Setan would go out into the camp teaching each new verse to all who would listen. He learned Scriptures, theology and doctrine in the mornings, and then spent the afternoons teaching what he had learned to others.

What an incredible team Setan and his pastor made! "I became a Pastor four months before I saw my first Bible," he said. Setan estimates that by 1980 there were about 35,000 Christians at Khao I Dang. They were a mixture of existing and new converts who were eagerly growing in their faith in Christ. Eventually they constructed a crude (by modern standards) but efficient sanctuary using bamboo poles with rice sacks stretched across them. It was appropriately named *The Church of the Lord Jesus Christ*.

It was while Setan was preaching on a Sunday morning that the unthinkable happened. He began his sermon on Romans 8:35. *"Who shall separate us from the love of Christ? Shall trouble or hardship or persecution or famine or nakedness or danger or sword?"* As he looked over the congregation he was horrified as he recognized a familiar face.

There she was – the very woman who had suffocated his friend by placing a plastic bag over her head for trying to slip a crab to Setan. As his eyes zeroed in on the hated woman, her body began to cringe as she recognized Setan and realized that he knew exactly who she was. "All those past feelings of hate and fear began to well up inside me," Setan painfully recalled. "Those feelings of revenge and revulsion almost took control of me. Then I asked the Holy Spirit to take control, and He did. As quick as lightning, God removed from me the spirit of bitterness, the spirit of anger, and moreover the spirit of revenge. He replaced it all with the spirit of compassion, mercy, love, and more importantly, the spirit of forgiveness toward this dreadful lady. I walked back to where the woman was sitting, knelt down before her and took her hands in mine. I told her that God forgave me; therefore, He wants me to forgive you for all that you have done to my family and friends. God will also forgive you if you ask Him."

She began to sob, but gave no reply to Setan's earnest plea. He returned to the pulpit. After that service, he never saw her again. "I pray to God that she made peace with Him," Setan said. "At least in my own heart, I knew I had forgiven her."

Setan continued to share his faith with anyone he could. He busied himself with working with the other pastors and training other young men to become leaders in the church. He had truly tried to lay aside the horrors of the past four years and concentrate on learning more about his Lord and Savior day by day.

~*~*~

Early in 1980 Setan began thinking seriously about marrying the woman he loved. But, the church elders at the camp in Khao I Dang still believed in arranged marriages, even for Christians. They approached Setan and said they had one certain woman in mind for him and his parents had agreed. Setan was very apprehensive because he had fallen in love with the young woman adopted by his family – Randa. However, being a good Cambodian, he was willing to accept whoever the church leaders believed was God's choice for him. He believed in and trusted their authority. He prayed it would be the one he loved, but he had to wait to find out.

When the church leaders talked to Setan's parents about Setan and Randa being married, they knew that there was one thing they had to take care of before they could give their consent. Prior to all the devastation and having to flee his country, Setan had been promised to another man's daughter. But because Setan's father was now penniless, that marriage was easily called off. Having no money was reason enough for the marriage to be cancelled, but the fact that Setan was a Christian was completely unacceptable in that family! This was certainly fine with Setan!

~*~*~

Randa Yos had caught the attention of the church elders and also Setan's parents. Randa had lost her entire family and was believed to be a perfect fit for Setan. She was only seventeen years old and had never considered falling in love. There was just too much to be done to think about falling in love, getting married and having a family.

Randa still dreamed of the day her family would stream through the camp gates and she would welcome them into her arms. However, she was convinced that going back to Cambodia was too great a risk at that time. "Every day I looked at the gate for them to come in," Randa lamented. "But they never came. Many nights I would cry myself to sleep, longing to be reunited with my family."

She still longed to save her family, and going to the United States would only prolong any chances of seeing them again. "It was like two persons inside my head," she recalled. "One was saying, if you go with Setan, you will never see your family again. The other was telling me to stay in Thailand in hopes of seeing them later or even going back to get them."

A short time later she learned that more than thirty members of her family had been killed by the Khmer Rouge. Her hopes of being with them again were further dashed. A wise man in the camp gave her some excellent advice. "Randa," he advised, "you must go on with your life. When you are strong enough, you can come back and save your family."

Randa had grown up a devout Buddhist with no concept of a personal relationship with a Living God. She was an angry, bitter young woman. However, she knew that if she got a chance to go to America she needed to learn English. She tried many places to get into a class for English lessons, but wasn't allowed because she did not have money to pay for the classes. One day she walked around the camp and found a place in an open area where they were teaching some English songs. She thought this was an English class and went in and sat down and stayed until it ended. As they ended the evening, the man leading the class announced, "We will see you tomorrow in this same place and same time."

Randa was anxious to get to the class the next day. However, to her surprise, the first thing they did was ask the people to bow their heads in prayer. Randa started to giggle because she had never known a class to begin this way. But, her desire to learn English was so intense, she was willing to do whatever they asked her to do.

To her dismay, they did not begin to teach English, but instead started to sing songs in English. This was followed by some teaching of the Scriptures in Khmer that this leader had memorized. Even though, this was not truly English classes, Randa continued to attend the meetings.

In those church services she soon found an unexplainable peace that permeated her whole being. Christian love was extremely evident all around her every time she attended these services. The more she went, the more she was attracted to the Christian love. She remembers that one of the songs they sang was very influential in her coming to faith in Christ.

We are one in the Spirit; we are one in the Lord. We are one in the Spirit; we are one in the Lord. And we pray that all unity may one day be restored. And they'll know we are Christians by our love, by our love. Yes they'll know we are Christians by our love."

Randa's new faith in Christ was guiding her now. "Before I knew Christ, I worried all the time," Randa explained. "I had such hate and revenge in my heart for the Khmer

Rouge and what they had done to my family and friends. I was so confused. Every day," she continued, "I would go to the church and learn more Scripture. With all the Scripture in my heart, when I prayed, I had such a peace that I cannot describe it. Eventually, I stopped worrying and put my whole trust in God."

The church also became a safe haven for Randa many evenings from the ruthless men in the camp who openly dragged young women out of their tents and raped them. Numerous times these deviates shamelessly raped the girls right in front of their families. Many girls became pregnant and had their lives ruined. Their families were too afraid to report the hooligans for fear of reprisals or further shame.

Every evening Randa and other young women would flee to the church for Bible Study. They would study near the altar while men in the church surrounded them to protect them, even while they slept through the night. In groups of ten, the women would pray for an hour while the other women slept; then another group prayed while others slept until dawn. Every night these prayer meetings took place and numbered as many as 100 women. It was interesting that these derelict men would pillage and rape, but would never enter a church to carry out their treachery.

~*~*~

As Randa thought back over all that had transpired while she was at this camp, she decided she should take the wise man's advice and go on with her life. Having grown to love Setan, she accepted his proposal, but asked if they could wait until they arrived in the United States to have their marriage ceremony. But Setan was anxious to make her his wife and didn't want to wait any longer. He convinced Randa to have the wedding there in the refugee camp.

On February 2, 1980, Setan and Randa were married in the first Christian wedding ceremony conducted in the Khao I Dang refugee camp. Not many people were invited to the small wedding, but hundreds curiously showed up. They were married by their Cambodian pastor and a British/Canadian missionary. It wasn't the traditional Cambodian three day ceremony with many gifts and incredibly large amounts of food that is so unique to Cambodians. It was simple and short.

Setan and Randa's Wedding Ceremony

Setan and Randa's Wedding (Feb 2, 1980)

"My British/Canadian missionary pastor walked me down the aisle," Randa said, "and the next thing I remember was the pastor saying, I now pronounce you man and wife. You may kiss the bride." They sipped an orange soda from the same bottle with two straws and shared cookies with their guests. "It was quite an experience," Setan proudly proclaimed.

A short time later, the entire Lee family all agreed that they must start over again in a new place. They were now ready to explore the opportunities available to them. Returning to Cambodia was unthinkable. The Khmer Rouge had taken control of all the country's banks, including most of Setan's father's assets. His father's partner had taken what money was left and deposited it in one of the Thailand banks in Bangkok. But, they knew that their Lord and Savior had a future for them somewhere else.

Chapter 6

PLANS FOR A NEW LIFE

꒜

WITH THE DECISION MADE THAT the Lee family would make a new start in a new place, they began making plans. They found that the United Nations Office had a directory of countries that would accept Cambodian refugees. The list included Australia, Canada, England, France, a few smaller European countries, and the United States of America.

The application procedure was relatively simple; write a letter to the chosen country's embassy and wait for a reply. For better odds, you were encouraged to write a request to all of the listed countries. But the Lee family decided that the United States was the only country they wanted to live in. Therefore, it was the only embassy they wrote to. Setan's reasoning was simple. "If you are a slave to the poor, their leftovers are nothing. But the rich, their leftovers are plenty and the United States was the richest country in the world."

Setan found a dirty piece of paper and scribbled as best he could the following letter over his father's signature.

My name is Chan Lee. Together with my wife and children, we have 14 people. We are survivors of the Killing Fields. We want very much to go to America. If you feel generously, compassionately toward us, please take us to your country.

Sincerely,
Chan Lee

That is all it said. Plain, simple and to the point! Boxes had been placed around the refugee camp which housed some 160,000 people. Applications for placement to a new country were to be placed in these boxes. So, Setan placed the tattered letter in a box for the American Embassy with hundreds of other requests and prayed that his family would be one of the few accepted.

A few days later they were contacted by the American Embassy. Mr. Chan Lee and all of his family would be moving to Aurora, Colorado in the United States of America! There, a local church would welcome them as part of a resettlement program. God is so good – all the time!

Soon after this, Setan and his extended family were moved out of Khao I Dang Camp and sent to Phananikum Camp near the capital of Thailand. There, they were to prepare the paper work for resettlement in America, and wait for it to be processed. Then final plans for their travel to Aurora, Colorado could be made.

~*~*~

While at Phananikum Camp, the family could do little but wait and pray. But Setan picked up where he left off at Khoa I Dang and began working with the Christians in this new camp. Before long, he was the pastor of a church of about a thousand believers.

Within that church there were more than 300 members who had their application papers rejected by interpreters at the U.S. Embassy. The papers were rejected simply because these applicants were Christians. Setan was very upset that these interpreters would refuse his parishioners the required papers to start a new life.

The congregation came to Setan seeking a solution to their problem with the embassy. Immediately Setan remembered Pastor Paul's last words before he left Khoa I Dang. He had simply said, "If you face any problems, whether big or small, you can always find a solution in the Bible."

So Setan instructed the congregation to pray that the Lord would direct him to a scripture passage that would resolve the language barrier. With limited Biblical knowledge and a great lack of Christian theological training, Setan placed the Bible on top of his head with the binding against his scalp. Using his index finger on his right hand, he put his finger into the Bible and asked God to lead him to a scripture for this situation. As he opened the Bible, it was at Mark 16. Setan's eyes fell on the 15th verse.

"And He said to them, 'Go into all the world and preach the gospel to all creation. He who has believed and has been baptized shall be saved; but he who has disbelieved

shall be condemned. And these signs will accompany those who have believed: in My name they will cast out demons; <u>they will speak with new tongues.</u>'" Mark 16:15-17 *(NASV)(*Underlining is added for emphasis.*)*

In the Cambodian translation of the Bible, instead of "they will speak with new tongues," it states, "they will speak a new language." This was just what Setan wanted to hear! None of his congregation spoke English at that time. With this scripture in mind, Setan asked for a volunteer from the congregation to allow hands to be laid on them to pray for the specific gift of English from God. This would allow this person to represent the people at the embassy. In just a matter of seconds, the congregation volunteered Setan to be that person! So Setan gladly accepted this. He then proceeded to give instructions to the people in how they should pray.

There were about 500 people who prayed all night, regardless of the curfew of the Thai authorities. At dawn the next day, Setan's head was still bowed and his eyes were closed in prayer when he felt that someone was standing near his face. As he opened his eyes and looked up, he saw a British missionary smiling at him with a brand new English Bible in his right hand. He began to communicate with Setan in English. Immediately, Setan responded to him in English! This was the first time in his life he had spoken English. The man asked Setan if he would like to have the English Bible. With a joyful heart, Setan replied, "Yes!" Setan began to read the gospel of John from Chapter 1 to 21, and read it twice that day. He was able to understand every single word of it! This assured him that God had honored the prayers of his people by providing Setan the ability to read, write, and speak in English. Within a short time, he became fluent in this new language. The people all praised God for His love and mercy. This was another miraculous gift from God!

Now it was time to step out in faith. Setan went to the American Embassy and applied for a job as an interpreter. His English being quite good, they hired him! Again, Setan, his family, and his parishioners realized that God was continuing to bless and provide for them.

One of the first things Setan did on his new job was to request that the Embassy consider reviewing those 300 rejected cases. He knew a lot of people were praying that the Embassy would listen to him with an open heart and mind. Once more, God answered their prayers. The request to review their cases was granted and ultimately all of the papers were approved for them to begin new lives in other countries.

~*~*~

Just five short months later, the Lee family was on an airplane headed for the United States. Their airfare was paid for by a loan they received from the Church World Services. The fare for each of the Lee clan was $350. Once on board the airplane, they all held hands and said a prayer of thanksgiving. This included Setan's parents, his three brothers and five sisters, two brothers-in-law, and his beautiful new bride.

The flight was bittersweet. They were leaving their home land probably never to return. Yet, they were on their way to an exciting new chapter in their lives that they were convinced only God could have orchestrated.

"We had all been through hell," Setan lamented. "Now we will taste a little bit of heaven."

As Setan and Randa pondered their past and their new life together, they made a solemn vow. "Some day, some how, we will do whatever we possibly can to help rebuild Cambodia – the forgotten land.

It is an established fact that the Lee family is the largest family to survive the Killing Fields and move to the United States.

~*~*~

Randa with her friends in Thailand

Newly weds Setan and Randa

Rarely in history has one group of people oppressed another so viciously and effectively as the Khmer Rouge did the Cambodian population between 1975 and 1979. The Khmer Rouge and the "killing fields" had claimed close to 3 million Cambodians. They were all victims of starvation, disease, slave labor – working millions of their countrymen to death, torture, execution, and murder. Many of these victims were Cambodia's educated and skilled workers, as well as their politicians and the military. Some of the most brutal and bloodiest attacks were against the independent and more moderate Eastern Zone group which was pro-Vietnam. One-fifth of Cambodia's population was annihilated by the Communist Khmer Rouge in three years, eight months, and 20 days! Prior to April 1975, no one would have believed nor could have even fathomed such an atrocity could take place in such a beautiful and peace-loving country.

Through their misguided beliefs in an agrarian socialist utopia, the Khmer Rouge murdered, tortured, starved, and worked millions of their countrymen to death in the Killing Fields and work camps; yet some miraculously survived!

Chapter 7

A NEW START

⋘⋙

IN NOVEMBER 1980, THE LEE FAMILY traveled to Colorado by way of Bangkok, Hong Kong, Alaska, and Oakland, California. As their plane descended over Denver, they thought the ground was completely covered with salt. Soon enough, they learned that the white stuff was not salt at all. It was a cold, powdery substance called "snow" that melted when it touched their hands! They had never experienced snow before in their lives.

Setan and Randa and their twelve relatives moved into the small basement of a Cambodian family's house in Aurora, Colorado (suburb of Denver). It was pretty crowded, but they were just grateful to be out of the refugee camp and still together. They were all amazed at how clean and gorgeous Colorado was.

Setan found a phone book and began to search for a church that would nurture their faith in Christ. He started by looking for a church called the Church of Jesus Christ – the same name as their church in the refugee camp. One listing was the Church of Jesus Christ of Latter Day Saints – the Mormons. That didn't sound right to him, so he kept searching and became more perplexed than ever.

"There were so many different kinds of churches! Baptist, Catholic, Lutheran, Methodist, Presbyterian," Setan explained. "So many denominations, and I didn't even know the meaning of the word *denomination*."

Setan soon met a man who did his best to advise Setan about the differences in various denominations. He pointed him to Faith Presbyterian Church in Aurora. Setan talked things over with his family and they prayed for God's guidance. The Lee family soon began attending this church and are still members there today.

About three months later, they were able to get a loan from that church and moved the family into a rental house, still in Aurora.

They quickly located the grocery stores, the schools, and the Good Will stores in the area, as well as the human services available for refugees.

The church helped Setan to eventually get his ordination through the Evangelical Presbyterian denomination. Later on, the church encouraged him to begin a church for Cambodian refugees, using their facility. Setan and Randa happily worked to establish this Cambodian speaking church.

Setan was the only family member who could speak English. He began to search for a job and was soon selected as a case worker for Church World Services, paying $800 per month. That was enough to cover the $450 rent on the house and all their expenses including food and clothing for the entire family. They were definitely very frugal people.

The state of Colorado required refugees to attend classes to learn English. However, they didn't provide assistance in getting to and from the classes. Setan already spoke fluent English, but the rest of the family walked each evening to Aurora Central High School for English classes. "It was a very long walk for my aging parents. They had to make this trek many times through the snow and icy cold weather," Setan recalled. "Many days they cried because it was so difficult for them. I felt so sorry for them." But, they all picked up some of the language very quickly and were so excited to be able to communicate with the Americans!

The local grocery store would give meat bones away to customers for their dogs. The Lee family would go into the store – all fourteen of them – and get a dog bone. They made some pretty tasty soup from all those dog bones.

As the family became more proficient in English, some of them were able to get employment at a local meatpacking plant. They combined the money they earned and furnished their home from a nearby Goodwill store. They purchased used clothing there also and even saved enough money to buy a used Volkswagen van. Setan was the only one with a driver's license, so he had to drive the family wherever they needed to go.

Mr. Chan, Setan's father, had a hard time finding work and felt so humiliated. In Cambodia he had been a very successful businessman as an importer-exporter. Now in his early sixties, he was turned down time after time when applying for jobs. "It was a very difficult time that I do not like to talk about," the elder Lee recalled. "But I knew God was faithful and would bring us through it together."

"It was a rough start," Setan stated. "But it was much better than living in the Killing Fields."

English hadn't come easily for Randa, but she was steadfast in her studies and graduated from Adams City High School in 1983 as a member of the Student Honor Society. She wanted to go to college, but knew it would not be possible for both her and Setan to go. So she set her mind to make sure Setan got a college education.

Randa did get her driving permit. Shortly afterward, she was driving her brother-in-law's car and crashed it into a house. She immediately jumped out of the car and ran to her own home where she hid under her bed, waiting for the police to take her to jail. Of course there was no jail for her crime, but she was cited for a traffic violation. She had to appear in traffic court, but thankfully the owners of the house and the judge were very understanding.

Not long after this incident, Setan and Randa rented an apartment in Commerce

City, Colorado. The Lee family wasn't really happy about this, but Setan felt it was time for them to move forward. They bought a used Mazda for $300. The car's heater didn't work and the window on the driver's side wouldn't go up. But Setan would bundle up and make the drive to his downtown Denver office in some very frigid conditions during that severe Colorado winter.

Randa's job search wasn't as sophisticated as Setan's. She found a job in a restaurant; however, the fact that she could understand more English than she could speak was a problem. As a result her boss placed her in the rear of the restaurant as a cook. Randa was still grateful for her $3.40 an hour which helped her and Setan very much financially. One year later, Setan changed jobs, moving to a Colorado State Government job dealing with thousands of refugees coming into Colorado from Southeast Asia and the former Soviet Union.

In 1985, Benjamin, their first child, was born. Did he ever change Setan and Randa's lifestyle! They both wondered if they would ever get to sleep all night again. But as they watched him grow day by day, little Benjamin was the joy of their lives.

Setan still dreamed of becoming a doctor, a profession he was pursuing before his captivity, but soon learned that medical school was much too expensive in the United States. Getting a loan was very difficult. To add insult to injury, American medical schools would not accept his credits from the Cambodian medical school he had attended.

"I was very discouraged," Setan recalled, "until I realized that God had another plan for my life." He soon began taking classes at Colorado Christian University, studying Christian theology. After graduation, Setan enrolled at Denver Theological Seminary.

Randa and Setan had the makings of a new and exciting life in Colorado. Yet, their hearts still burned to return to their homeland and help their fellow Cambodians. With their tremendous growth in Christ, they could offer more than just physical help for their countrymen. Now they could offer help that would make a difference for eternity!

But how could they possibly achieve such a noble humanitarian task? They barely made ends meet financially and a trip back to Cambodia, plus all the supplies they would need to carry, appeared to be an insurmountable undertaking. How in this world could they possibly find the resources needed to meet such a challenge?

"We knew that returning to Cambodia during our lifetime was probably a remote possibility," Setan said. "But we also knew we served a big God and that all things are possible through Him. We had no idea it would come as quickly as it did.

Chapter 8

HOUSE ARREST!

❖

THE INDEPENDENT EASTERN ZONE group that was so very pro-Vietnam had fled into North Vietnam when the Khmer Rouge extended their "cleansing purge" to the people in the eastern parts of Cambodia. But they had not wasted time while in Vietnam. It was this group, along with Vietnamese leaders, that later formed the core of a government that was established in Phnom Penh in 1979. When the Vietnamese rolled into Phnom Penh, they drove the Khmer Rouge into the jungles. This effectively ended the genocide, but Cambodia was greatly weakened by isolation from the Western world and the US sponsored embargo against the Vietnamese. The economy was at an all time low, causing a vast famine that drove thousands into refugee camps along the Thailand border.

War had broken out between the Vietnamese and the Khmer Rouge. Then in 1984, the Vietnamese drove the Khmer Rouge into Thailand. The Khmer Rouge's response was to use guerilla tactics, laying thousands of land mines in any area that would deter the movement of supplies into Cambodia. The Vietnamese retaliated by laying mines from the Gulf of Thailand to the Laotian border. The economies of both Cambodia and Vietnam were in absolute shreds. All of this plus a number of other outside factors finally convinced Vietnam to withdraw all its military troops from Cambodia in 1989. Needless to say, the government of Cambodia was in utter disarray and very unstable. The economy of both countries suffered tremendously.

The people of Cambodia had nothing with which to begin rebuilding their country. There was great poverty and most Cambodians felt utterly helpless and disillusioned.

~*~*~

It was during all this upheaval that Setan made his first effort to return to his homeland. He flew to Thailand in 1988; however, he was not allowed to cross the Cambodian border. He tried again in 1989 only to be denied again. During both attempts to enter his native country, while he waited for permission to enter Cambodia he did not let the time go to waste. He was able to minister through preaching and training leaders in the Cambodian refugee camp along the Cambodian-Thai border. But soon, he had to return to the United States both years.

That same year Randa's brother and sister found their way to Denver and were reunited with her. They knew where their grandmother was located in Cambodia, and they also knew where to find the rest of Randa's surviving family members, including her sisters who were still alive. After thinking most of her family had been killed, Randa was ecstatic!

Soon after her family's arrival, Randa gave birth to her second child, Sandra Chanda Lee, on September 8, 1989. She was a beautiful baby girl. It was easy to see that she looked very much like her gorgeous mother! This had certainly been a busy year for the Lees and they felt so blessed to have more of their family around them in Colorado.

In January 1990, while Setan was still working for the U.S. Government, he collapsed at work. His major symptom was sharp pains in his stomach. He was brought by ambulance to Saint Joseph Hospital in Denver. There they discovered that his appendix had ruptured and he had severe infection. The doctors took him immediately to surgery to remove the appendix and to deal with the infection. But things did not go well. Tubes were put in place to drain the infection, and strong antibiotics were given to him intravenously, but they just were not taking care of the horrible infection. He was unconscious for the next 30 days. During this period, only Randa and their pastor were allowed into the intensive care unit. Days passed as Randa sat, watching and waiting for Setan to wake up. But, after nearly a month had passed, Randa was informed by a group of doctors that Setan's chance of survival was extremely slim. They advised that she should begin making arrangements for the inevitable. Randa was extremely distraught as she thought about what the doctors were telling her.

While Setan was in the hospital, 3-month old Sandra had been fighting a severe urinary tract infection. Soon, baby Sandra was so sick she was taken to The Children's Hospital (which was just a few blocks down the street from Saint Joseph Hospital). Randa couldn't understand why all this was happening. She was so torn about where she needed to be, she could hardly function. But even in the midst of all this, she was praying to her Lord. Her strong faith brought her strength when she needed it most.

Randa refused to accept the doctor's advice in regard to Setan's condition. She believed that the *God of the Universe* who had spared Setan's life in the killing fields would never take him home before he finished what God intended him to do. God had called them to go back to Cambodia, preach the Gospel, and help the poor people. Randa asked her church family to join her in prayer for another miracle in the lives of Setan and their daughter. God honored their prayers by bringing Setan back from the brink of death yet another time! Baby Sandra also soon recovered and was back in her mother's arms.

Setan was still in the intensive care unit when he woke up from the comma. Shortly afterward, he heard the news that Cambodia was slightly opening the doors for outsiders to come into the country. Regardless of his condition, Setan got all excited. But even in this excitement, he was questioning why God would let the doors of Cambodia start opening at such a time as this. From the time they left Cambodia and came to the U.S., it had been in Setan's heart and in his prayers that God would let him be among the first to return to Cambodia with the Gospel message when the door of opportunity opened. Why didn't this door open when he was healthy? Why would God not answer his prayers and grant his heart's desire?

Even though Setan was still hooked up to all the tubes and oxygen, he told Randa and their pastor that he would return to Cambodia in the next few weeks. His mind was made up! He truly believed that God would enable him to do this. Randa was astonished and felt extreme agony; she thought that all the fever and infection had affected his thinking. She reminded Setan that he was still in the intensive care unit. Just how did he think he could make a trip to Cambodia that quickly?!

However, Setan's plans were moving forward with what he knew God wanted him to do. He challenged the doctors to release him from the hospital sooner than they really wanted to. He had to sign a form stating that he was taking responsibility for his own health. If anything went wrong, the doctors would not be held responsible. So, he left the hospital and began preparing to go to Cambodia.

Two weeks after Setan left the hospital, he and Randa made a very difficult and agonizing decision. Knowing the risks they were taking to go back to Cambodia at that time, and realizing that they could be detained or worse, they didn't feel they could take their children with them. Wanting the best for their children, they took them to the church and placed them on the altar. They requested that someone in the church take care of their children while they made their trip to Cambodia to carry out God's calling on their lives. Immediately, a couple walked to the altar and said that they would take Benjamin and Sandra Lee into their home. What a blessing it was to realize that this couple were both physicians — Doctors Jim and Glenda Singleton. Setan and Randa informed the Singletons that if anything happened to them while they were in Cambodia, they might have their children for the rest of their lives. Legal documents were prepared to ensure that their wishes would be carried out if indeed they didn't return from Cambodia.

As they prepared to leave their children to do God's Will, they found a verse of Scripture in Ephesians 3:20-21 which became very real to them during the following days.

"Now to him who is able to do immeasurably more than all we ask or imagine, according to His power that is at work within us, to Him be glory in the church and in Christ Jesus throughout all generations, forever and ever! Amen" (NIV)

~*~*~

A short time later, Setan and Randa both attempted to get into Cambodia. Because Setan had been denied entrance into Cambodia from Thailand in both trips he had previously made, they decided to try crossing from the Laotian border on the east side of Cambodia. As soon as they reached the immigration office in Laos, they learned that they had been denied visas into Cambodia. However they remained relentless in their mission.

"We had come this far," Randa explained, "and we were not taking 'no' for an answer!"

Once they reached the border of Cambodia, they told the truth; they were searching for relatives and had come as missionaries to spread the Gospel of Jesus Christ. The border guards were very suspicious. When the word "missionary" was mentioned they immediately arrested Setan and Randa as CIA agents. They were taken to the capital city of Phnom Penh and were placed under house arrest.

They were back in their native country for which they had longed for more than ten years. *They had finally made it, only to become prisoners again – just as they were before they had escaped!* What in the world was God up to? Setan cried daily, but not because they were in prison. He knew that the authorities would eventually discover they were not spies. His tears were shed because he and Randa were being detained from their mission of finding relatives and spreading the Gospel of their Lord and Savior Jesus Christ.

"I wept for my people," Setan explained. "The whole country was in such a dismal state."

The once beautiful buildings in the capital city had been burned to the ground or badly damaged during the war. The airport where they were now under house arrest had bushes and undergrowth higher than Setan's head. The airplanes were sorry excuses for flight purposes and in desperate need of repair.

Not only were public buildings and landmarks destroyed, most private homes had suffered the same fate. While under house arrest Randa had learned that her family's beautiful home in Battambang had also been reduced to rubble, and, so had most of the other homes in that city.

The Capital city had fared no better than the airport. There was no electricity, food was scarce, and jobs were few and far between. Only a few vehicles traveled the roads that were riddled with potholes and in great need of repair. Homeless orphans aimlessly roamed the streets.

Most of the men had been conscripted into the Army. As a result, most of the inhabitants of the cities were women searching for food and work. To say that things looked hopeless in Cambodia at this time was a tremendous understatement.

Even in the midst of despair and travail, a Christian's hope reigns eternal. That hope was uppermost in the minds of Setan and Randa.

While they were still under house arrest in Phnom Penh, members of Randa's family came to visit them. They were not at all certain that they would be allowed to see Randa. But a compassionate guard at the airport where Randa and Setan were being held allowed them to visit her. At last she was reunited with her grandmother, mother, two sisters and two brothers.

"It had been ten years and I hardly recognized them," she said. "They had been out of work and were dressed so poorly. But it was so wonderful to see them again." The visit was much too short and her family had to return to their home, still uncertain of what would happen to Randa and Setan, or if they would ever be able to see them again.

After two long months, Setan and Randa were freed by the government authorities with no explanation for their being detained. They didn't wait around to demand an explanation, but left immediately without asking questions. "I think they just got tired of us," Setan quipped.

As they left their place of detainment, they were almost aghast as they walked along the city streets. Everything was filthy; garbage and trash was everywhere. "There was some help available for the children," Randa recalled. "But the women for the most part turned to prostitution just to stay alive or to feed their families. I resolved in my heart that when I returned home to the United States I would do all within my power to help these women free themselves from prostitution and become alive in Christ."

Setan and Randa remained in Cambodia for another month after they were released from house arrest. During that time, they became aware of some underground worship services being held in the area. Setan diligently preached the gospel in those churches and encouraged them to remain faithful.

Setan preaching in an underground church

As they prepared to leave Cambodia, Setan and Randa could do nothing to get her family members to the United States, except for her mother. Because the United States was still accepting parents of resettled refugees, they were able to help her leave Cambodia to make her home with them in Colorado.

~*~*~

Setan and Randa returned to Colorado and Setan resumed his job with the Colorado Health Department. They were grateful that his job was still available. But within a short time, they made a decision that would again completely change their lives. Setan felt strongly that God was leading him to return to Cambodia to evangelize and disciple the people of Cambodia for Christ. He and Randa had lengthy discussions about this and they prayed earnestly to be certain they were correctly hearing God's call on their lives. They consulted with a number of Christian friends and sought their prayers and advice. They knew that beginning an ongoing ministry in Cambodia would not be easy and they couldn't even imagine how this would come to pass. They did realize, however, that this was a huge undertaking!

When they felt absolutely certain that this was God's will for their lives, Setan began taking the necessary steps to carry out this calling. He announced their plans to their Cambodian congregation which met at Faith Presbyterian Church. Their family members were also part of that congregation. He then announced their plans to the pastor of Faith Church and to their many prayer partners.

A short time later, Setan quit his job at the Colorado Health Department to begin making his arrangements. Even though she was a bit nervous about Setan being gone for long periods, Randa would remain in Colorado to raise their children and work to support her husband's calling. She did not hesitate to take on her role in this calling.

"This is our mission," Setan explained. "If we do not answer God's call to Cambodia, who will?"

Both Setan and Randa's family feared for his safety, but they were Christians and prayerfully supported their decision. After all, each one of them believed it was God's will for Setan to return to Cambodia; therefore, God would take care of him.

Thus, Setan returned to Cambodia, alone, to begin the work for which God had been preparing him all of his life – to help his people, physically and spiritually.

What would he encounter upon returning to his homeland? Where would he start? How would he fund his new mission? Were strict Cambodian Buddhists really ready to hear and respond to the Gospel? These and many other questions permeated Setan's mind on his thirty hour trip back to his native land – the Forgotten Land.

Chapter 9

KAMPUCHEA FOR CHRIST

꙳

WHEN SETAN RETURNED ALONE to Cambodia in the latter part of 1990 to begin his work among his native peoples, he did not realize he would not return to America for three years. He missed his wife and family greatly, but returning to Colorado was just too expensive, especially for a young missionary living on less than a shoe-string budget. He also feared he might have difficulty, if not downright rejection, getting back into Cambodia if he visited his family in America. So, he would stay until God provided the means to go to Colorado and safely return to Cambodia to continue the work.

During those first months, Setan spent most of his time traveling the countryside planting new Christian churches in every village and town that would welcome him. This was a tremendous challenge, but day by day God blessed his efforts. A little later on, he set up a small office in Phnom Penh that would be the hub of his mission thrust to his country. This small compact office would also serve as his sleeping quarters. His ultimate goal at that time was to establish a training school for pastors and other church leaders. He knew he had to have leadership and pastors to shepherd the people in these new churches. This school was so needed, and Setan felt that God would provide it in His time.

In due time, Setan took a job teaching English at the local university. It didn't pay much, but it was something. This job also provided an opportunity to be around college students—the foundation for the rebuilding of his country. This was very encouraging to Setan.

On May 1, 1992, Setan helped establish the Phnom Penh Bible School (PPBS). This was a huge step, because it would help train the Christian leaders he so much needed for the small churches he had established.

Setan was very pleased to see young men and pastors studying the Bible and learning God's instructions and guidance in a classroom setting. However, his native country did not always see his work as being good for the Cambodian people and did not make his work easy. Several times he was imprisoned for short periods because of their lack of understanding what he was trying to do for his country. But God was faithful and both the school and his other work continued.

Setan leading at Phnom Penh Bible School

In January of 1993, he returned to Cambodia after a brief visit in the United States. A few weeks after his return, he wrote to the people at Faith Presbyterian Church in Colorado about an incident that occurred when he arrived in Cambodia.

"I was met upon arrival at the Phnom Penh airport by the National Front of the Communist Party. They had obtained my picture from the Foreign Ministries Division who issued my visa. They tried to persuade me to leave the country on the next plane. Yet, God is good. I was able to enter the city, although the Government of Cambodia took my passport away for about two weeks. They were accusing me of bringing American (Western) influence into the country. There were several other accusations which caused some delay to my work."

He continued, "God was, and still is, on our side. Through your prayers and God's grace, I was filled with the spirit of boldness to face the problems. The Spiritual battles were very real. I met with the Minister of the National Front (the third highest government official in Cambodia) and defended myself with the Word of Truth. I convinced the government official that my real mission was to bring the Light into the dark world. My passport was returned to me soon after our debate! Praise God!"

When the pastor of Faith Presbyterian Church received this message from Setan, he telephoned him. He explained that the Mission Committee had already set up the mission budget for the fiscal year; however, the pastor told Setan that he would go to the committee and ask them to put Setan into the mission budget by faith. The church had not been aware of all Setan and Randa were doing in Cambodia. After the pastor's plea, they added two new missionaries, Setan and Randa Lee, to their budget and they are still a part of their budget to this day!

In 1994, Setan's partner in starting PPBS was killed in an airplane crash. It had been overwhelming for Setan to continue his work at the school and keep doing the other ministry he felt God called him to do before his partner died. Now it was even more difficult without his partner. He was emotionally, physically, and spiritually drained. But he was determined that he would at least continue his work as Director/Teacher until he saw his first class graduate.

~*~*~

Setan and Randa had taken every bit of their meager savings to answer God's call to the people in Cambodia. Randa worked feverishly in Colorado to support and sustain her husband and take care of her children. She was employed at a factory doing assembly line work as much as sixteen hours daily, including Saturdays. Added to this were the duties of motherhood that could not be neglected—cooking, cleaning, arranging babysitting schedules, car repairs, house repairs, and anything else that needed to be done.

"At first, I was real scared about doing everything without my husband," she recalled. "But I knew the importance of our mission in Cambodia and that spurred me on. Did I ever get depressed or lonely? Absolutely! But I couldn't even think about quitting what God had called us to do. Besides, I did have family and friends who would help if I needed it."

However, it was Randa who mowed the lawn and shoveled the snow at their home. She did the laundry, paid the bills, and all the other things a mother has to do. "It was hard, because I had depended on Setan a lot," she said. "But I had to depend on myself now."

There was no mail system in Cambodia, so Setan and Randa exchanged letters through a Red Cross friend who made frequent trips to Cambodia. Randa would write of what was happening with the children and their families and Setan wrote of the progress with their mission. Occasionally, though few and far between, they would speak to each other by phone. "Separation was tough," Setan explained, "But our resolve and faith in God was tougher. God kept our marriage strong."

Randa and the children, Benjamin and Sandra, would visit Setan in Cambodia during their summer vacations. They had no choice but to reside and sleep in Setan's office. "It was difficult and expensive," Setan recalled, "and the tiny office was very crowded with all four of us jammed into it." At one point, they considered moving the family to a neighboring country like Thailand or Malaysia. But the cost of living there, coupled with the price of education for their children in a foreign country, made that prospect virtually impossible.

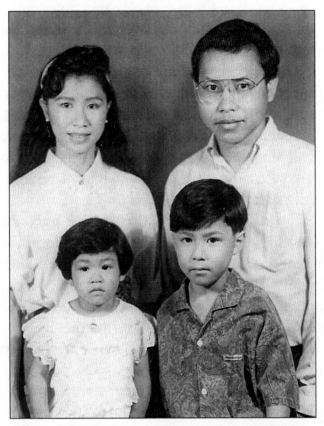

Setan & Randa with Benjamin & Sandra

Randa and Setan had continued to pour their personal money into their mission work and the financial load was really heavy. After much prayer about their finances, they decided it was time to share their vision with others who might be interested in investing in

God's work in Cambodia. By this time, Setan had been in Cambodia over three years. He later returned to Colorado for short periods of time whenever they could afford the airfare so that he could work at raising money in the United States, or wherever God led him. They really believed that God would provide what was needed to spread the gospel and to help take care of the people in his native land, and take care of their family.

Randa continued to dream and pray for a building that would be a safe place for women who wanted to leave prostitution; a place where they would not only be housed, but fed, clothed, given medical help, and educated so they could provide for themselves. She wanted this home to have electricity and other modern amenities so these young women could thrive as they were learning. They would be trained in trades such as cosmetology, seamstresses, and computer skills to give them life skills to improve their family's well-being. Randa began saving all her overtime pay in the hope that someday her dream could become reality.

All the hard work, all the prayers, and all the sacrifices began to pay off. God was providing day by day for the ministry Setan and

Randa lived for and these provisions made them strive even more to fulfill His calling. They continually sought for God's guidance to continue building the visions He had given them. Setan was still carrying his duties at the Phnom Penh Bible School, but he knew he would have to let go of those duties before long. It was just too hard for him to be there the required time to continue this work and still do the other things God laid before him. They began praying for God to provide the expertise they needed to begin an organization that would be pleasing to God and help them to fulfill His call. Setan had worked diligently in Cambodia for about five years by this time.

~*~* ~

In 1995, God provided seven co-workers who would come along side Setan to help raise funds, give spiritual guidance, and hold them and their work up in prayer. They would help him create an organization that was both legally and spiritually sound. Setan was thrilled to see God work through him and these men to establish an organization to help reach the nation of Cambodia for Christ.

On the morning of July 8, 1995, Setan witnessed the graduation of the first class from the Phnom Penh Bible School. At that point, Setan resigned his position at PPBS to concentrate on the other ministries in Cambodia.

That afternoon, with the support of these seven co-workers, Setan founded *Kampuchea for Christ (KFC).* This organization would provide the assistance and backing for their mission work in Cambodia. The goal of the organization was to support Setan and Randa and help raise funds for the various ministries they envisioned. This was a huge step forward! Setan and Randa were, at last, seeing God bring into being the organization they had hoped and prayed for.

The first goal of KFC was the establishment of a Ministry Training Center. There they would train and build up a group of equipped evangelists, church planters, and pastors who could take the gospel to the country of Cambodia. They realized that this would take time to come to fruition, but they began making the plans for the training center.

Phnom Penh Ministry Training Center

Over the next two years, they trained 38
men to become missionaries in their own
country. Setan worked closely with them and
they successfully planted 48 churches around
the country. Without the Ministry Training
Center this could not have been accomplished. These Christians were taught to evangelize, pastor these churches, and minister
to the people using their diverse gifts from
the Lord. Setan had felt from the beginning
that KFC had to set their aim on building all
aspects of the church, including evangelists,
worship leaders, church planters, and what-

ever else was needed to reach the people of Cambodia.

"My Dad always taught me," Setan explained, "that before you can invite others to join you in a business, you have to show them you are serious and have invested much of yourself into your own business. When they believe in you and what you are doing, they will then invest with you." Dad was right. And, God had answered their prayers right on time!

Chapter 10

A DREAM REALIZED

꩜

SINCE THEY HAD LEFT THEIR homeland, Randa had continually prayed and dreamed of a center to get women off the streets and train them to be women of God. It had to be a place where the women would feel safe, because they would come from the brothels and byways where their families had sold them, or they had been forced into prostitution. Randa had seen the fear and desperation on the faces of these women and she couldn't get them off her mind. The years of waiting seemed long, but she felt sure that God had placed this burden on her heart and it would someday come to pass.

In 1996, a long awaited call finally came from Setan in Cambodia. "Randa," Setan said, "I have found the place for the *Women's Center*. It will cost $3,500. Do you have it?"

"I'm not sure," Randa hesitantly responded. For the past six years she had hidden her overtime money all over the house in vases, in books, under pictures, in drawers, between mattresses and other inconspicuous places. She had stashed as much as $300 at a time. "I knew if I put the money in a bank," she recalled, "I would have borrowed it and then never paid it back for the women's center. That's why I hid the money all over the house."

She tried to recall where she had hidden each stash over the years as she searched the house. As she found the money, she took it into the seclusion of her bedroom. There she prayed as she opened each receptacle to divulge its contents. As she sat on the floor counting the cash, her heart jumped with joy as she passed the $3,500 mark and she still had more to go. When it was all counted, it totaled more than $6,000 – more than enough for the two and a half acre site Setan had located! The property was in Kampong Chhnang, the provincial capital, fifty-five miles north of Phnom Penh. Randa's heart sang as she visualized her dream finally coming true! She joyfully sent the entire $6,000 to Setan through a trusted friend who was going to Cambodia.

Setan was ecstatic as he purchased the property a short time later for the long awaited Women's Center. His heart was full of praises as he thought about how God had provided funding for not only the Women's Center, but much more. He realized that money Randa had "squirreled away" all those years was enough to also purchase property for another ministry. "Wow! God is so good, all the time!"

However, nothing was easy in Cambodia in those days. Setan soon learned that there was a problem with the Women's Center property. It was located in a dense jungle at the edge of the city that was infiltrated with landmines. The mines would have to be cleared before they could begin construction of the buildings.

Cambodia still has one of the worst land-mine problems in the world. More than eighteen thousand Cambodians have been killed by landmines and another forty thousand have lost limbs as a result. Clearing the mines was an arduous and extremely dangerous under-taking. At that time, it was accomplished by individuals, often spouses of victims, lying prostrate in the dirt, covering the entire area by probing with a knife or blade to locate each mine. When a mine was discovered, it was usually detonated on the spot. Setan and Randa realized that this would take a lot of time, but the land had to be safe before they could even consider building on it.

They both knew that purchasing and clearing the land was just the beginning of seeing their vision realized. By now, it had been about two years since Setan had purchased the land. They continually prayed for God to provide enough funds to build at least one building so they could begin to rescue these destitute women.

In 1998, Randa returned to Cambodia with the leaders of Global Opportunities for Christ, Bob and Sandra Emery. Through the influence of Mr. and Mrs. Emery, an anonymous donor from New Zealand donated $25,000 toward construction of the much needed building. It was an exciting time. Randa would have liked to remain in Cambodia to see the construction of the building. But she had to return to Colorado about a month later.

As soon as possible, construction began on a two-story building made of concrete. On completion, it was painted a tan color. This was a dream come true for Randa and Setan. It contained a kitchen, offices, and larger rooms that would be used for classes during the day and sleeping quarters at night. Setan soon began hiring employees. One of the new employees was a relative of Randa who was still living in Cambodia.

The women's center was named the *New Development Center* (**NDC**) and was opened for the first girls to occupy it in 1999. Setan and other church workers had rescued twelve prostitutes from the streets and placed them in the center. There they received shelter, three meals a day, medical care, training in personal hygiene, Christian counseling, Christian discipleship, and sewing or cosmetology classes.

New Development Center

At first the work was very difficult. The women were not as pliable as Setan and the staff had hoped. They begun to understand that they would have to be won over to the Gospel little by little, certainly not overnight. The girls all had a very strong Buddhist background. KFC soon realized that they were also facing some serious medical problems as well—lice, yeast infections, worms, tooth decay, and many of the young ladies tested positive for AIDS. Some of the girls were addicted to a cheap form of methamphetamines that caused them sleeplessness and eating problems. This had been forced on them so they would be able to service more men in the brothels.

But the physical problems were greatly overshadowed by their mental scars. These women were outraged with anger—anger for the life they had been forced into accepting. Very few had voluntarily become prostitutes. Many of them were forced into it by being sold by their parents; others had accepted it just as a way to stay alive. Some of the aids infected girls were so angry they wanted to go back to the brothels and have sex with as many men as possible in the hopes that the men too, would be infected with the AIDS virus.

The AIDS virus began to take its toll. The center's first counselor and Bible teacher personally nursed the first two women in her home until they died. She constructed crude wooden coffins for each and built a fire to consume their earthly bodies. She then took their ashes and buried them behind her house in graves marked by simple wooden crosses.

In spite of all the efforts Randa, Setan, and the staff put forth, of the original twelve women who were taken into the New Development Center, none survived. All of them died of AIDS. By this time however, each one of them had heard the gospel and accepted Jesus as their Savior. They are spending eternity with God because of Randa and Setan Lee's God-given vision!

"It was so sad to get to know these women, to laugh with them, to cry with them—all the while knowing they were going to die very soon," Setan explained. "It broke my heart."

"Even though we knew they were going to die," Randa lamented, "It didn't mean we shouldn't help them. There still is so many that need God's love. We can't help them all, but we can help some."

~*~*~

These problems were not the only things that plagued Randa and Setan that first year. In November 2000, Setan wrote an email to his KFC board explaining the situation at the NDC. One of the key leaders at the center had not been faithful to his task and had not been truthfully accountable for the funds that were entrusted to him. It was difficult for them and the KFC board to learn that their trust had been misplaced. "We are still in transition," he wrote. "We are changing our leadership and finalizing the paper work for the center to be legally operated without restrictions from the local authorities." (Not having all the paper work completed had caused some restrictions during the first year of operation.) "Now, we are in the process of recruiting more women for our Center. Currently we have only one woman left at the center. All the others have died of AIDS," Setan wrote.

Despite all the problems they had encountered, Setan reported to the KFC board that 94% of the building project for the NDC was completed by the end of November 2000. His goal was to have the total project completed within a few more days. This was a huge accomplishment.

A few U.S. churches and Christian organizations began helping with funding toward the operation of the NDC, which enabled them to bring more and more women out of the sex trade. A few teams of short term missionaries also began to come along side to help with whatever tasks they could accomplish. Setan and Randa thanked God for all these provisions.

The women's center was requiring a lot of time, but Setan continued to travel to Phnom Penh frequently to keep the training going for the pastors and leaders of the churches they had founded. He was always grateful when a pastor from other countries could come to Cambodia and teach at a conference for these young men.

He had also been working to bring much needed medical help to the people of Cambodia. He had been in contact with several doctors in Singapore, the United States, and South Korea to get their input on how this could be accomplished. With their help, he led teams of medical people and pastors to areas of Cambodia that most needed their help. Thankfully, these teams would bring in large quantities of medicine, medical equipment, and other supplies in order to maximize what they could accomplish among these poor people.

From time to time, there were still military conflicts that flared up around the country. On November 23, 2000, Setan and Randa sent an email to many of their partners and prayer warriors and asked for their prayers. They wrote:

"Cambodia is once again facing some political crisis and we need a lot of prayers and petitions to the Lord God Almighty. Many streets in the capital city are blocked by heavily armed soldiers and police officers.

Parents have come to get their children…We ask that you hold our people and nation up to the lord; that His kingdom would reign here in Cambodia at this critical time…"

Thankfully, God answered their prayers and the conflict lasted only a few days, but this kind of crisis was not uncommon in Cambodia.

The work at the women's center continued. God was blessing the various ministries of Kampuchea for Christ around their country. Many were coming to Jesus through the preaching of the gospel and their many other evangelistic outreaches. When Randa returned to Denver in December 2000, she arrived with a grateful heart for all the answered prayer. God had made her dreams a reality!

Girls at NDC preparing for baptism

Chapter 11

PREVENTION AND MORE

༄

THE DAY IN, DAY OUT MINISTRIES to the ladies at the new Development Center (NDC) had made Setan and Randa realize that there needed to be a way to prevent girls and young ladies going into the sex trade. For the women in the NDC, it was too late to prevent all the suffering and horror they would experience. But, they wanted to find a way to save other girls and young women from being trapped in the horror of the sex trade. They began to pray that God would show them how they could meet this need. Both Setan and Randa believed that this was the desire of God's heart too; that He would show them how to prevent as many ladies as possible from ending up at the NDC, or worse yet, dying in that horror on the streets.

God answered their prayers in a most unexpected way. The offer they received was not exactly what they had thought it would be, but they knew it was a gift from the Lord. They received word that several of the Colorado Rotary Clubs were interested in helping them open a Trade School to teach young people some skills that would enable them to become a useful part of the Cambodian infrastructure. This would take a lot of planning, hard work, and cooperation between the KFC board, Setan and Randa, and the leaders of the Rotary Clubs. Also, the plans had to be communicated to all the Rotarians involved, and a budget had to be established to determine the cost. Even though it would not be a school owned and operated entirely by KFC, the entire board felt this was a big first step in helping to save some young ladies from the sex trade. God worked in many different ways to accomplish His will – that was certain!

On May 1, 2001, two years after the NDC was built for rescued women, Kampuchea for Christ (KFC) opened the *Battambang Trade School (BTS)* with 40 students in conjunction with the Colorado Rotary Clubs.

Here, they would provide job skills to the girls *before* they got into the sex trade. For two years, they rented two flats in downtown Battambang with the help of the funds from the Rotary Clubs. This help came with some certain guide lines KFC must follow. The school was designed to stimulate the Cambodian economy and give a valuable education to young ladies who were too poor to attend school elsewhere. The intent was to educate teenage girls in sewing skills to provide them with a good source of income so they could provide for themselves and their families. The sewing program was designed to sufficiently train the girls in one year.

Soon, another benefit from this new trade school was realized. Cambodian children and young adults could not attend public schools unless they wore school uniforms. Most families could not afford to purchase the uniforms, so their children could not attend school. The teachers and students at the trade school made it a part of their studies to make school uniforms and donate them to these poor families. More than 300 uniforms were made and distributed during the first three months of the school year. This was indeed a tremendous blessing and filled a great need.

Several months later, Setan learned about a piece of land nearby that was for sale. It had been the Battambang city dump. After looking at this property, God began to give Setan a vision of converting this dump into a beautiful piece of property for His glory. As he spoke with Randa about this vision, they realized that they still had some of the money that she had saved earlier. It was just enough for them to purchase that land! Now, they needed buildings!

By this time the BTS was no longer being funded by the Rotary Clubs, but the classes were still meeting in the rented flats. Since it now was completely under the leadership of KFC they could begin to conduct Bible study classes and other Christian activities with the students.

Another first for the school quickly followed. They expanded the curriculum to include computer training classes. For these classes, they charged a small fee which would pay for this training and also help sustain the sewing classes as well. Immediately, both classes were well attended by girls from very poor families and young ladies who had no way to provide for themselves. Most of them also attended classes that taught the gospel of Jesus Christ, and the majority of them accepted Christ as their Savior within a reasonably short time. The school offered a one year program and then graduated the students. God had blessed them tremendously.

Setan and Randa looked back at this point and realized how God had so graciously provided, step by step, the answer to the prayers they prayed while they were working among the girls at NDC. Already they were graduating students who would become a useful part of their communities rather than ending up in the horrible life of prostitution and abuse. They were no longer so vulnerable to being kidnapped or sold.

The need to put buildings on the land God had provided for the BTS was now paramount. There was so much potential here! So, Setan returned to the United States to help raise the needed funds.

Shortly after he reached the U.S., he had the privilege to speak at Bethesda Community Church near Dallas-Ft. Worth, Texas. He shared the vision God had given him for the Battambang Trade School. They needed to fill the Battambang dump land and build a multi-purpose building, a conference center, and a church there. Rev. Des Evans was the

Senior Pastor of the church, and Rev. Charlie Salmon was the Mission's Pastor. They quickly caught Setan's vision. They stated that by faith, they were trusting God for this vision for the dump land to become a reality.

A few months after Setan spoke to that congregation they informed him that they had raised more than $30,000 to fill the land and to build the multi-purpose building. What a tremendous blessing and answer to prayer! In 2003, Bethesda Community Church sent a team of twelve men under the leadership of Pastor Salmon to Battambang. This team started work on the multi-purpose building, providing tremendous leadership in getting this project accomplished.

Battambang Trade School

Meanwhile, Setan and Randa drew funds from their 401K and also built a little house on that land. They lived in this home to oversee all the construction for the new Trade School campus, and to ensure a smooth transition from the rented flats into the new multi-purpose building. The little house they built is still used by the BTS Director.

A few years later, some land which had a building already on it became available. It was located next to their new multi-purpose building. Some business men from Florida generously helped KFC to purchase this property. This provided BTS with the much needed expansion to enable them to help more rescued girls and more children with uniforms.

This was truly answers to Setan and Randa's prayers, as well as those of their many donors and prayer partners. Day by day, they began to see more of their visions become reality. At last the ministry would not only help prevent young ladies being caught up in the horrific sex trade, but also to provide training for them to work toward rebuilding the infrastructure of Cambodia.

KFC also found a way for BTS to help the children in the area have a better opportunity for education. Among all their other duties, the staff of the Trade School began supervising the distribution of school supplies. In one year alone, they distributed 30,000 items to children who could not afford to buy them.

The Lees felt that there was still a lot more that could be done through this Trade School. They especially felt it would be a big plus to have English classes taught by an American. In 2008, God sent a young man to fill this position. He was there only one year, but the English classes he began are still being taught.

Battambang Trade School was, and still is, a very important link in accomplishing several aspects of the visions Setan and Randa have for their ravished homeland. God has provided so far, and He can be trusted with the future of this school!

Chapter 12

AWESOME ANSWERS
TO PRAYER

৵৵

IN LATE SUMMER OF 2001, GOD ALSO led Setan in another amazing direction. Setan was working with the National Director of Kampuchea for Christ in Cambodia and the director of evangelism. These were native Cambodian men that Setan had led to Christ and trained to come along side him as KFC reached out to the people of Cambodia. Both of these men were also pastors of one of the churches KFC had planted. They were praying and planning their strategies for their future ministries. Setan was very grateful for these pastor friends who worked so diligently with him.

As they prayed together, Setan's mind was on more than just the plans they were making. He began to explain to these pastors that he believed he was being led by God to go visit the President of the Khmer Rouge. His pastor friends thought Setan was absolutely crazy to even consider this. No one had made such a visit and lived to tell about their experience, and they believed Setan would be no exception. But Setan insisted that when God told him to go, he must go. They all knew this would be a dangerous endeavor, but seeing Setan's resolve to go, they all joined in prayer and began brainstorming to determine how to approach this God-given assignment.

After much discussion and prayer Setan suggested to these trusted friends that they would go to Pailin, which was an area still occupied by Pol Pot and his men, and ask for permission for him to see the President. "If I am to see the President, they will grant permission. If not, I will not attempt to go," Setan told them. A very simple plan, but would it work?

Shortly after that meeting, Setan and his pastor friends traveled to the western part of Cambodia near the Thailand border. This was definitely an adventure of spiritual growth and faith stretching. It would stretch Setan's own faith to what he believed was close to its limit.

When they approached the city gate, there were about fifty armed guards sporting AK-47s on their shoulders and all wearing the dreaded black uniforms. Needless to say, Setan and his friends were extremely fearful, especially since one of his pastor friends was a former Khmer Rouge officer. They were told to exit the vehicle and the soldiers thoroughly searched it. They were also subjected to a full body search and questioned as to what their business was in this town. Setan responded that they just wanted to visit the town because it was so beautiful.

After several minutes of discussion, the Khmer Rouge spokesman returned with their answer. Setan and his friends would be allowed entrance, but only until three-thirty that same afternoon.

They entered Pailin, the fortified stronghold of the Khmer Rouge, at about noon. They were all very hungry, but there were no restaurants immediately in sight. Then they spotted a place that appeared to have food, even though there were no signs designating it as a restaurant. They entered the open air house and sat down at a table. To their surprise they found themselves completely surrounded by Khmer Rouge soldiers. Suddenly, one of the soldiers at another table sprang from his seat and began to salute Setan's table.

"We had no idea what the soldier was up to," Setan recalled, "and really did not know what he was doing." Moments later they realized that the soldier was saluting one of the pastors. He remembered the pastor as an officer who was formerly very prestigious in the Pol Pot regime. The soldier then asked the pastor if he was there to see Brother #3. The perplexed pastor turned and looked at Setan. Setan responded, "Sure, that's exactly why we are here today."

Brother #3 (actually the Khmer Rouge President) was the title given to the man who was third in command of the Communist regime just under Pol Pot himself. What an incredible answer to prayer! This was how they would get see the President! One of the soldiers immediately left a nearby table, saying he would return. About fifteen minutes later he came back and said, "Comrade Khiev Samphan is expecting us."

This was unbelievable! Off they went, arriving across town at a small inconspicuous house. Setan and the pastors were told to remain outside until they were informed for sure that Brother #3 would entertain them. They huddled around each other and began to pray that God would take charge of their possible meeting and that they would be His, and only His, mouthpiece.

After several minutes passed, an older man with gray hair exited the house and approached the praying pastors. He motioned for them to come into the house. They soon realized that the gray haired man was Brother #3, himself, the President of the Khmer Rouge. He was now in his mid-seventies and very frail. Comrade Samphan seemed very edgy and not at all comfortable with the pastors. And, he had every reason to be uneasy, because he was in hiding. There were many courts of law that were waiting to bring him to justice for his crimes against his fellow Cambodians. Setan tried to sit down close to Comrade Samphan, but was motioned to sit on an adjoining couch. He tried his best to build a relationship with this man, but he was resisting almost every word that came out of Setan's mouth. Setan began by stating his respect for the man, even citing the good reports he had heard of him when he was a child and growing up under Comrade Samphan's government. Setan even told him that he had great admiration for him and all he had done for Cambodia.

Setan went on to explain not only the good he had heard about this new friend, but also told him that not everyone is perfect. "We all have faults," Setan told him, "including you, Mr. President." He didn't go into great detail for he could see that Comrade Samphan was getting more and more uncomfortable. Setan was trying to set up an opportunity to share the gospel of Jesus Christ. He spent the next forty-five minutes vividly describing just who Jesus Christ really is and why He came to earth to die for each of us.

After Setan's explanation of the Gospel, Comrade Samphan began to show incredible interest and even allowed Setan to have his picture taken with him. When they first arrived, Setan had asked for a picture to be taken with the President, and he very reluctantly granted permission. In that picture he had kept his distance from Setan. Now, however, Comrade Samphan leaned closely toward Setan. He had obviously gained a new friend.

The President didn't make a decision for Christ that day, but he did ask Setan to leave some booklets and gospel tracts for reading later. He also asked if he could pray the sinner's prayer at a later time without Setan being present. Of course Setan provided him with Christian literature and explained that he could pray that prayer at any time. Setan wrote on a piece of paper the steps for Comrade Samphan to pray and ask Jesus to come into his life. He also wrote what to do after he prayed the prayer. Comrade Samphan asked Setan if there was a particular place he needed to pray the prayer. Setan told him he could do it in the house, in the backyard, or even in the bathroom. He explained that the place doesn't matter, only the attitude of his heart.

It was getting close to three-thirty and Setan knew he must leave. Before he left he asked Brother #3 if he could arrange a meeting with the military leader of Cambodia who was in hiding in northern Cambodia. Comrade Samphan asked why he wanted to meet with the general of the Khmer Rouge. Setan explained that he wanted to share the same good news of Jesus Christ that he had just shared with him.

Comrade Samphan explained that such a meeting would be difficult to arrange and the trip there would be even more difficult. It would take at least three to six months to arrange such a meeting and the journey there would be very dangerous because of many landmines dotting the road. The visit would be very risky Comrade Samphan warned, because the general was very moody and prone to outbursts of anger. Setan was not dismayed and assured Comrade Samphan that he was ready and willing to go at any time. They left his home not having any idea what to expect next.

About three and a half months passed and it was now early in 2002. One afternoon about three o'clock, Setan's phone rang. It was a call from an assistant of the military leader of the Khmer Rouge who was still in hiding in Northern Cambodia. He told Setan that permission to see the general had been granted, but he would have to be ready to leave the next morning.

As Setan hung up the phone, his mind was spinning. On the one hand, he was very excited that God was going to allow him to share the gospel with one of the most feared military leaders of the world. On the other, he sensed a fear for his life that he hadn't experienced since the days of the "Killing Fields."

"I knew the evil one was pouring everything into my mind that might hinder me from going. I understood that was the reason for the fear I felt," Setan explained. "At the same time, I knew the Lord had answered my prayer and I must act accordingly."

Chapter 13

A MOST POWERFUL WEAPON

❦

SETAN HUNG UP THE PHONE AND called his National Leaders who had been waiting as anxiously for this answer as he had. "I told them the news I had just received," Setan recalled. "I asked them to pray fervently for my journey and requested that they also ask their congregations to do the same." Neither of them was happy about this. "I could hear their pleas," Setan recalled. "They were screaming into the phone, no, no, we don't want you to go. It is too dangerous and you are putting your life in jeopardy!"

"I explained to them that for more than twenty years I had been praying that God would allow me to witness to the Khmer Rouge. Why not witness to the dreaded military general?" Setan said. "I can not go back on my promise to the Lord." Setan and his friends knew that this general was Pol Pot's "right arm" man. He was the one who carried out Pol Pot's every command.

"Here's the deal," Setan explained to his partners in the gospel, "I will leave in the morning. And please don't call my wife or my children and tell them what I'm doing. If you hear from me in two weeks, I'll obviously be alive. If you don't, then I will see you in heaven."

Setan's partners continued to cry as he spoke of all he knew about the coming days and shared his anxiety about what he didn't know. He tried to make them understand. What he truly knew was that he must obey God rather than men and prepare for whatever his lot might be. He rested in his faith in God's divine providence for his life.

The next morning Setan was waiting at the appointed place when two Khmer Rouge soldiers arrived dressed in black. They were riding double on a 50cc Honda moped with AK47s slung over their shoulders. They also had several hand grenades attached to their uniforms.

They informed Setan that he was to take nothing with him but the clothes on his back. He pleaded with them to allow him to take his Bible. They searched through the Bible thoroughly and asked if it had a weapon hidden inside.

"It has no hidden weapon," Setan told them. "However, it is the most powerful weapon that any man can ever own."

Obviously they did not understand what Setan meant. They asked why he needed to take this book. Setan told them that he liked to read and he was going to be gone a long time. "Reading is how I best spend my time on long trips," he explained. So they agreed to allow him to take his Bible.

Setan climbed aboard the Honda seated between the two young soldiers. The driver pedaled the moped to start the engine and the long journey began. They left about six-thirty in the morning and arrived at the general's camp at seven thirty that evening. To say it was a rough ride is putting it lightly!

The road was a military road made of grass and dirt and covered with trees. In many places they had to dodge landmines.

When they weren't dodging mines, they were scouting ahead for undiscovered ones. In many areas they had to dismount the Honda and carry it around, through, or over obstacles in the road.

There were times when Setan needed to take a rest and he asked to stop, but the soldiers didn't grant his requests. They admitted later that they were afraid he might try to fight them and leave them stranded. Of course Setan had no weapon to fight them, and he didn't understand their wariness. They were two – he was only one.

As he arrived at the general's small hut, he saw nothing inside but a few flickering candles. It was then that Setan began to feel very fearful for his life. Surrounding him were several soldiers with weapons, all staring at this stranger coming to visit their commanding officer.

Setan trembled, his mind unsettled as he contemplated the man inside the small hut. The general was responsible for the death of millions of people. Now Setan Lee was about to meet him in person.

"I knew from his reputation that if he did not like me," Setan said, "I could be killed on the spot and carried out to be buried."

"I told myself that this could be the end of my life," Setan said. "I was not feeling like a super Christian ready to give up my life. Instead, I was full of fear for my life."

Setan slowly walked into the hut where two of the guards didn't bother to raise their heads and acknowledge his presence. The general's wife took a quick peek at Setan and then lowered her eyes to the same position as the guards. Only a small girl, the general's daughter, looked at Setan and followed his every move. The air was so thick with tension he could hardly breathe. It was so quiet he knew he could have heard a pin drop. At that point, Setan knew he had to turn the whole situation over to the Lord. "Lord, please take control," he prayed.

"Everything I had learned in Bible classes, seminary, Sunday School, Evangelism Explosion, and evangelism seminars," Setan recalled, "but my mind went completely blank. I couldn't remember a thing. I just told the Lord to take charge. I didn't know where to begin and where to end. And I thank God that I did that, because otherwise I knew I was in deep trouble."

Setan sat in a chair waiting to be told when to speak. The general was in a rage banging his hand repeatedly on a table. With each bang Setan's body shook with fear. The general was saying, "I can't believe that he left me in such a position. I'm frustrated, so frustrated. He failed me, he failed me."

The Holy Spirit began to take control of Setan and he reached out his right hand toward the general. As Setan's hand touched the general's shoulder, he said, "I'm sorry, so sorry. Who failed you? Who failed you?"

The general replied, "Who else, who else? Pol Pot! I have followed him for many years and now I am in my sixties. I have done everything for him and now he is gone. He has left me. He is dead! All of these soldiers are looking to me and I have no directions."

Setan quickly interjected, "I'm so sorry Mr. General, but I have good news for you. I know another individual, a close friend of mine who is very faithful. He has never failed me. He is very trustworthy. As a matter of fact he is the most powerful man you will ever meet."

For the first time in the meeting, the general made eye contact with Setan. "Who is this person?" the general inquired. "Who is he?" he asked loudly.

"I told you," Setan stated, "He is a very powerful man."

"Is it the President of Cambodia?" the general asked.

"No," Setan responded, "He is powerful, but it is not him."

"Is it the prime minister?"

"No, the prime minister is powerful too," Setan said, "but his power is limited. The individual I want to introduce to you is much more powerful than any of these people."

The general looked intently into Setan's eyes and said, "Please, please, tell me who this person is!"

Setan, gaining more boldness in his faith with each passing moment responded, "General, I'm not going to tell you unless I know you seriously want to know Him."

The general instantly responded, "I am serious!"

"His name is Jesus Christ, the Lord of the Universe, Setan told him." Setan then proceeded to lead the general to a personal relationship with Jesus Christ. "The power of God in that place was amazing!" Setan stated.

In a short twenty-four minutes, this powerful general was brought to his knees by the Gospel of Jesus Christ. And not only him, but his wife and daughter along with him. The general asked Setan if there was room for him in God's army. He said, "I have served Pol Pot for many years, now I want to serve Jesus Christ."

The general began to call Setan "teacher" which also means pastor. He went outside and told all of the guards that they were free to go. They were no longer needed to guard him. The general was a new man—a new man in Christ. He now had a personal relationship with the most powerful God in the universe.

Chapter 14

GOD IS GOOD – ALL THE TIME!

❦

A S SETAN WENT TO BED THAT night, he was very much at ease. He had obeyed God and the result was new life in Christ for several people. However, he didn't sleep very well for it was one of those hot, humid evenings. He had to sleep under a mosquito net which cut down immensely on the little bit of breeze available.

Before he went to bed, the general had made another request of his new-found friend. "Teacher," the general stated, "Tomorrow, I want to introduce you to a group of very special people."

Setan answered that it would be a great honor to meet these people. In Setan's mind he was thinking that the general was going to introduce him to another general or some other dignitary in the Khmer Rouge. He didn't want to insult the general by inquiring as to who this might be, so he politely told the general that he was looking forward to meeting these special people.

The night seemed to last forever; morning could not come soon enough. Setan rose very early from the little sleep he'd had. Soon the General and his wife were awake too.

After breakfast, the general and his wife took Setan to meet the general's special people. Setan pondered who they could be. They walked quite a distance into the jungle. All of a sudden the general and his wife stopped and the general began to call children out from the jungle. They seemingly came from everywhere. Some were dressed in threadbare clothing, but most with no clothing at all. Who were all these children approaching them?

"Teacher," the general proudly said, "these are children whose parents died during the war and I am very sad to say that I cannot take care of them, even though I feel responsible for them."

Setan's heart sank within him because he knew the general was going to ask him to take care of these very needy children. He also knew there was no way he could care for them. The General stated that there were more than three hundred of these extremely deprived children living in the jungle like animals and they so desperately needed help from someone. "I wanted you to meet some of them," he told Setan.

Setan explained that there was absolutely nothing he could do to help these children and that he could not promise them help in the future either. He thanked the general for the introduction. Setan, the general and his wife left the jungle to return to the village. As he walked out of the jungle, Setan's heart was heavy, but he had no plan or means to help these children way up here in this jungle.

That day Setan was introduced to other generals and Khmer Rouge officers and they all heard the Good News of Jesus Christ. Many of them accepted Him as Lord and Savior. Setan felt so honored that God had answered his prayers to witness to the Khmer Rouge.

Soon it was time to try to sleep again in the unbearable heat. Thankfully, another Khmer Rouge general who owned a larger house invited Setan to stay with him. Setan was pleased and felt he would be more comfortable there. He retired for the night.

Before long, something incredible happened in that room. There was no electricity in this entire village and what occurred caught Setan completely by surprise. "It was as if a big television screen appeared right in front of my face," Setan recalled. "In big bold letters and numbers it read: James 1:27." I immediately grabbed my Bible and looked up the Scripture reference.

"Religion that God our Father accepts as pure and faultless is this: to look after orphans and widows in their distress…"(NIV)

Setan was agitated at reading this and became very frustrated with God. He asked that God take this sign away from Him. He felt that his plate was just too full to take on another ministry; especially a ministry so far into the jungle and away from civilization. He mentally wrestled with God and told Him that he was there just to witness to the general, which he had done. He was not there to start an orphanage.

Much to Setan's relief, the screen disappeared, but for only a few minutes, then it came back. That vision would return many times throughout the night. Now, it wasn't the mosquitoes and the heat keeping Setan awake. It was a message from God and he did not want to receive it. As the morning appeared, the picture finally vanished much to Setan's delight.

The morning of the third day, Setan asked the general if there was any where he could make a phone call to his office in Battambang. The general told Setan that they would have to walk over the mountain into Thailand and make an international phone call to his office.

Setan and the general left almost immediately for the trek over the mountain into Thailand. It took a few hours, but soon Setan was talking to his pastor friends and explaining that he was still alive. He told them all that had happened to their new brother in Christ and his family and the other Khmer Rouge soldiers.

When Setan had finished his news, one of his pastor friends said, "Setan, I need to tell you something." Setan explained to him that this call was very expensive and that he needed to speak quickly. He had only about seventeen dollars and the call had taken almost all of his money. The pastor answered that he understood and he would speak as fast as possible. Setan's fellow pastor exclaimed, "I didn't sleep all night because James 1:27 kept appearing in front of my face and I don't know what it means." Setan was absolutely amazed and yet at the same time, relieved.

"What a coincidence," Setan retorted, "You and I need to ask God's forgiveness for not heeding his message and for being so stubborn and fighting against Him. I had the same vision. We must listen to God. I'll be in touch with you soon."

Setan went back to see the general and explained what had happened. He asked if he could bring the other two pastors up to join him to discuss how they could start an orphanage for the children in the jungle. The general was more than happy to know that Setan was considering the plight of the jungle children.

Before long, Setan and the other two pastors traveled into the deepest part of the jungle of Cambodia to answer God's call to begin an orphanage. As a result of that visit to the Khmer Rouge stronghold, a new church was established. (There are now seven churches in that jungle.) The general and his whole family were baptized, attesting further to the power of the Gospel to change lives and work miracles.

~*~*~

Setan and his pastor friends had spent a good bit of time in the jungle among the soldiers and the children as they scoped out their God-given task. They knew that God had a plan, and they were praying for guidance and wisdom. They knew they needed a lot of money, and they believed that God would supply all that was needed in His time and in His way. They were excited about what God would do in that jungle, but still not exactly sure where to begin.

By the time they returned to the city of Battambang Setan was very sick. They soon learned that he had contracted a serious case of malaria. His temperature reached 107 degrees and hung there for several days. They took him to Phnom Penh where Setan admitted himself to a hospital. The doctors told them that they didn't think Setan would survive. After several days in the hospital, Setan lost all hope that he was going to recover and accepted the fact that he was probably going to die and go meet his Lord.

His Christian friends visited him frequently and spent most of their visit in tears because they, too, thought he would die. "I just asked the Lord," Setan recalled, "to allow me to see my wife and children one more time before I died." He managed to dress himself and was taken to the airport to fly home to Colorado. He dared not tell airline officials that he had malaria for they would not have allowed him to fly. He did an amazing job of acting like a perfectly healthy man, even though he still had a very high fever. He knew it was going to be a very tough performance for the twenty-five hour trip from Cambodia to Colorado, but he was determined to see his family one more time.

When Setan arrived at the Denver International Airport, he was so weak that he collapsed and was taken directly to the hospital. After the doctor examined him, he told Setan that there was very little chance that he would survive this serious bout with malaria.

Setan didn't want to die in a hospital, so he asked the doctors if he could go home for his last days. The doctors granted his request. Two volunteer Christian nurses began to visit him for daily treatments. They gave him regular sponge baths in cool water to help bring the temperature down. Setan felt certain that he was in the last days of his life before going to meet his Lord.

Chapter 15

GOD'S MYSTERIOUS WAYS

❧

JUST WHEN SETAN BELIEVED EVE-rything was under control and that he would die in peace surrounded by his friends and family, God had something else in mind for him. Setan's doctor had predicted that the treatments for malaria would be unsuccessful and that he would die within a few weeks.

David, Setan's 19-year-old nephew came by every day to help take care of him. He stayed by Setan's side as his temperature again rose to about 105 degrees. He helped his uncle for many hours each day in any way he could. Setan was so grateful for David's care and attentiveness that he began calling

him son (the greatest sign of affection possible in the Cambodian culture.)

Setan had been home for about a week, and
was resting quietly at home in his own bed,
preparing to leave his family and go home
to his Lord. Setan and his young daughter,
Sandra, were home alone on August 3, 2002,
when the telephone rung. Sandra answered
it. The news she would bring to Setan would
shake him to the very core of his being.
Something had happened that would change
his life beyond his imagination. "Daddy,"
Sandra screamed amidst her tears, "David is
dead!"

Setan was very feverish and was experi-
encing chills. He had been disoriented all day.
When he heard Sandra's words, he exclaimed,
"Sandra, what on earth are you talking about?"
He asked Sandra to get an adult to come into
his room, but she told him that everyone else
was gone. Setan managed to dial the phone
number of his older sister's home, but when
the receiver was picked up, all he could hear
was uncontrollable weeping and wailing.
He was trying to make sense of all he was
hearing. After pleading for someone to tell
him what had happened, he got someone to
calm down enough to talk with him. He was

horrified to find that Sandra's statement was true. He too began to weep.

David had drowned in Lake McConaughy in Nebraska where he had gone with some of his friends who had recently graduated from High School. Setan cried out to God, "Lord, I'm supposed to be the one to die, not David! Why David? He's only nineteen and had his whole life ahead of him. Why him, and not me?"

Setan had not realized that during the time he was screaming at God, his fever was dissipating very fast. It was completely gone within a few time, but that fact completely escaped Setan. He got dressed and drove to his sister's house where he found his family sobbing as never before.

He still found it impossible to believe that his nephew was actually dead, so he picked up the phone and called the sheriff at the lake in Nebraska to verify the tragic news. After talking with the sheriff and being told that the young man that had drowned was indeed David, Setan hung up the phone, still in disbelief.

David Hou, Setan's nephew

"We had lost so many family members in the *Killing Fields,*" Setan stated. "I just couldn't grasp this news. Something like this was not supposed to happen to us here in the United States." But it had, and Setan believed that this loss might be too difficult for a family as fragile as his own to comprehend at this time in their lives.

"Later, as I was lying in bed, still crying," Setan said, "I was shouting at God." He recalls asking God, "Why did you take David instead of me? He was so young and had his whole life ahead of him."

Since Sandra had given him the news of David's death, Setan had not thought about himself. He had just done what he felt he had to do. Now, he suddenly realized that at the very time he learned of his beloved David's' death, his malaria had been healed! The fever was gone.

As this realization filled his mind, Setan felt that God was speaking to him. It was not an audible voice, but God was filling his being with a message. It was as if God was telling Setan that He had taken one son away, but had given him hundreds more – that every child in Anlong Veng was now Setan's child. Setan knew that God was saying, "I'm bringing David home and giving you his name for the new work I want you to do." Setan knew the name for the big project for the children in the jungle in northern Cambodia was now confirmed—The David Project.

Truly O God of Israel, our Savior, You work in mysterious ways. Isaiah 45:15 (KJV)

~*~*~

Anlong Veng is a jungle village very near the northern border of Cambodia. It was still populated by the Khmer Rouge, and because the rest of Cambodia greatly feared and hated them, the area was virtually cut off from the rest of the country. It wasn't difficult to understand why they were the poorest and most illiterate people in Cambodia. Because of the hard life of these people, both in the years past as the Khmer Rouge soldiers ravished their homes and land, and now as they struggled to survive. Many parents had died or abandoned their children. It is estimated that there was over 300 orphans in the jungles of Anlong Veng.

As the KFC board members worked along side Setan, they estimated that they needed about $200,000 to fulfill the first phase of the vision Setan, Randa, and the two Cambodian pastors had for the orphanage. Setan and Randa's teenage son, Benjamin, soon caught the vision of his parents and was filled with compassion for all those orphans in the jungle. He talked at length with his parents about how he could help raise the money to build the much needed orphanage.

Benjamin was a member of Interact, which is the Rotary International's service club for young people ages 12 to 18. Interact clubs are sponsored by individual Rotary clubs, which provide support and guidance, but they are self-governing and self-supporting. They could draw members from the student body of a single school or from two or more schools in the same community.

Benjamin took David's project to his Interact Club and asked if they would work with him to raise whatever money they could to help build the orphanage in Anlong Veng. Benjamin knew that each year his club was to complete at least two projects – a community service project, and at least one project that would further understanding and goodwill internationally. He was excited when the club took the orphanage as one of their projects.

That year, they were able to raise $13,050 to help build the David Center for orphans! Benjamin's compassion was contagious. The members of Ben's Interact Club had worked hard and God blessed their efforts greatly.

Original David Center Project

In December of 2004, Setan reported in his newsletter:

"David's Center, the orphanage in Anlong Veng, has finished its first phase of construction – the kitchen and dining hall are completed and the first story of what will hopefully become a three story dormitory is also finished – and KFC's staff is currently seeking out the neediest children in the area. By the end of the month, KFC hopes to have the first group of children at the orphanage. David Center at this time can house only 24 children...Pray for the staff that they will be led to the children most in crisis, and that they will know the best ways to minister to these children who are not only physically in need, but also emotionally and spiritually.

"The second phase of construction will be the two additional stories of the dormitory, and after that we are planning on building one more three-story dormitory, and two three-story classroom buildings...We pray that one day David Center will be able to care for every single one of these children in the jungle."

The David Project later became the David Center Orphanage. The vision is still for it to be a haven for all those destitute children in the jungle who have no place to turn. It is a refuge where these children can learn to grow physically, mentally, socially, and most of all, spiritually.

Today, the original plan for the David Center Orphanage buildings has changed somewhat. But God has provided three two-story dormitories, a meeting hall for classes and worship services, etc., a building for showers and toilet facilities, a building that houses the directors of the orphanage and a guest room, and a new kitchen and dining building (completed in 2009). It also has a deep well for fresh water and also a prayer tower. There is still no electricity in Anlong Veng, but a gasoline generator supplies power for their computer classes, their evening meetings and other things needing electricity.

David Center Orphanage 2010

When the David Center Orphanage was built, KFC was the only organization seeking to minister to the children in this area. Even though there is upwards to 300 children without parents in this jungle, David Center can house only about 65 children. KFC hopes in the near future to have facilities for at least 120 of these children as God provides to build additional dormitories.

There is a couple who are the directors ("Dad and Mom") to these children, and a staff of about 12 who take care of the children, cook for them, see that they get to and from school and do their home work, teach them the rudiments of sanitation and personal hygiene, teach them English, and most importantly, teach them the Love of God and lead them to a personal relationship with Jesus. These children love to sing about Jesus and they meet every day to worship Him. The staff there has a big job, but it is very rewarding!

Many of the first children who were brought to the David Center Orphanage have now finished the schooling available there, and have been moved on so they can attend high school, or have been sent to Battambang Trade School to learn a skill. It is the hope of Setan and Randa, and the David Center directors, that every child who comes to the orphanage will leave knowing Jesus as their Savior and having skills that will enable them to find work to support themselves.

Setan and Randa know that God is good— all the time. They lean firmly on verses like Romans 8:28 now more than ever.

"And we know that God causes everything to work together for the good of those who love God and are called according to his purpose for them." (NLT)

David's Center Orphanage is dedicated in the memory of David Hou whose life was cut short at Lake McConaughy in Nebraska that much fruit could be born from him, following the ultimate example of our Lord and Savior. Jesus said in John 12:24:

"I tell you the truth, unless a kernel of wheat falls to the ground and dies, it remains only a single seed. But if it dies, it produces many seeds." (NIV)

Chapter 16

STEP BY STEP AND DAY BY DAY

꙳

THE OFFICES OF KAMPUCHEA FOR Christ (KFC) are located in the Capitol City of Phnom Penh. This is where Setan and Randa have their "home" in Cambodia, and where they work or rest as they oversee their ministries, and launch new ministries or evangelistic outreaches. It is where their financial office is located, and a large meeting room where they meet with pastors and church leaders for training and leadership meetings. Setan works diligently to continually increase the knowledge and leadership skills of the pastors and leaders of the 57 churches and 87 home cell groups they have planted around Cambodia.

It is interesting to know how God provided the Headquarters for KFC. Even this was truly miraculous. From 1990 when Setan had first gone back to Cambodia, they had rented various facilities to use as a church, their Head- quarters, and other ministry purposes. When the rent was raised beyond their means, they would rent another place. After a number of years, they began to strongly feel that they needed a permanent place and to put down roots for the work of KFC. They talked to the Lord about this, and asked for His guidance, but they had no idea how or when this would become a reality. As always, God worked in mysterious ways.

One day in late 1997, someone brought a letter from an American broker which stated that Setan and Randa were to receive an inheritance in the form of bonds from Mrs. Edith Merritt Best. They were both shocked at this news, because they had no idea that Mrs. Best could or would leave anything to them. She was an American "foster" grandmother to the Lee Family after they arrived in the United States in the 1980s. She had been a real blessing to all of them over the years.

Setan and Randa were very humbled as they learned the details of this dear lady's gift.

Grandma Best's instructions were that the approximately $15,000 was to be used to purchase a home in Cambodia for the personal use of Setan and Randa Lee. It was not a gift for the KFC ministries; this bequest was for the explicit purpose of providing a home for them. To say they were surprised didn't begin to express their feelings and excitement.

The more they thought about the gift, the more they felt they really needed a headquarters building for KFC more than a permanent place to call home. After much prayer and discussion, they asked Mrs. Best if she would please allow them to use the funds to purchase the much needed HQ building that could also house their church in the heart of Phnom Penh. But her response was that her gift was only for a home for them.

Setan began to use every reason and excuse he could come up with to change her mind. She still replied that her original instruction to buy a permanent home was to be carried out.

Setan and Randa continued to pray. Setan sent pictures and videos, trying to convince Grandma Best to change her mind, but to no avail. Then he sent some drawings of the buildings they envisioned to convince her to allow them to use the money for a place that would be part home and part Headquarters. As Setan and Randa waited for her response again, they prayed earnestly for God to change Grandma Best's mind. When they finally received her response after the drawings they sent, she gave in to their request! They were so thankful to her for understanding their passion. Setan located a building and purchased it for exactly $15,000.

A short time later, the pastor of Colorado Christian Fellowship in Aurora, Colorado, Rev. Phillip Smith, Jr. and his wife, Dr. Sylvia Smith, came to Phnom Penh to teach at the Bible Training Center. While there, they saw the need to expand the KFC Head Quarters property. An expansion would not only allow them more home and HQ space, but they could house a church also. The church had been in Setan and Randa's original hopes. The land and building along side their current property was for sale and acquiring this would double their space. Pastor Smith told the Lees that he felt God would have them invest their faith in the KFC ministry. Again, God supplied their need from an unexpected source! They purchased that additional property and building for $20,000. KFC now owned two buildings – one for their personal use, and one for the HQ and a church. To God be the Glory!

~*~*~

It is Setan and Randa's hearts desire to continue to evangelize and win people to Jesus in the city streets, and in the jungle villages. Urban evangelism is perhaps the most difficult and multi-faceted ministry of Kampuchea for Christ. "There is so much drug addiction, so many gangs, prostitution, superstition, great poverty and great wealth, all mingled together making a thick darkness through which very little light shines," Setan stated. Yet, KFC has made great headway in many cities by organizing any kind of mass communication possible to reach the people. They host crusades and concerts, air television and radio programs on local and national stations, and print gospel tracts for distribution. Through all of this, KFC has been one of the most successful evangelistic organizations in Cambodia.

As the Lees reflected on the amazing and miraculous things that had happened over the years, they knew only the Lord of the Universe had the resources and the power to bring all this to pass. Setan and Randa continued to step out in faith and carry out every vision that God gave them, one by one. The work was not easy, but they continually praised God for all He was accomplishing day after day; year after year.

~*~*~

In early 2007, Setan and the KFC board began to see the possibility of their ministries reaching beyond the Cambodian borders. They felt that they should change the ministry's name to accommodate what God would be doing in the future. Also, Kentucky Fried Chicken had opened their first restaurant in Phnom Penh, which quickly became known as KFC, causing some minor identity problems. But the main reason for the name change was that Kampuchea is the word for Cambodia, and when the ministry expands into other Asian countries, it couldn't be called "Cambodia for Christ." Therefore, they all agreed that the name should be legally changed to **Kampuchea for Christ, (dba) TransformAsia.** This became a legal reality in October 2007, and the organization is now generally referred to as **TransformAsia or (TA)**.

April 2007 was the 32nd anniversary of Khmer Rouge's attack on Cambodia. During that attack and the following four years, almost all of their educated and professional people were killed. During this anniversary period, Setan felt the call of God upon his heart to build the first Christian University in Cambodia. He even located the site where he felt God would have the University built. Later that year, TA was able to purchase this land for this University. Soon afterward, the architectural drawings were completed. The huge job of raising the funds for the buildings is still underway.

This university is to be a Christ-centered place of higher education preparing students for success both professionally and personally. Plans are to offer degrees in Humanities/Religion, Medicine, Business and Counseling. The university should produce Cambodian leaders who will impact churches, business, politics and medicine.

In June, 2007, Setan wrote in his newsletter, "A lot has been accomplished in the last few weeks that I've witnessed. Thanks to God and His Son Jesus Christ that a harvest is still coming in through your sustained prayers and support.... and God is working mightily in Cambodia."

In the latter part of 2007, Setan wrote the following in his newsletter, "Remember how the upper class of Cambodia perished by the hands of the Khmer Rouge between 1975 and 1979. We lost most of an entire generation of people and now God is giving me the vision to build this University to train and equip 1,000 pastors/leaders and to plant 1,000 more churches. We not only need pastors and evangelists, but we also need Godly leaders for the people and nation of Cambodia. Please pray for this adventure and very important project!"

"Be careful for nothing; but in every thing by prayer and supplication with thanksgiving let your requests be made known unto God."
Philippians 4:6(KJV)

"But my God shall supply all your need according to his riches in glory by Christ Jesus." Philippians 4:19(KJV)

~*~*~

For ten years, Setan worked with Musicianaries, an organization that was headed by singer Bobby Michaels. Being a gifted singer and fundraiser, Bobby's organization worked with Setan each year to purchase up to 300 tons of rice and went into cities and villages where the Gospel had not been preached. They did many evangelistic concerts around the country each year, reaching many who had never heard the name of Jesus before. When Bobby sung, he presented the gospel by testimony as well. They also distributed about 50 pounds of rice to each family that needed food. Other musical talent such as the Continentals, or Miss Melanie Steenkamp, a singer from South Africa, usually joined these evangelistic concert tours. Thousands of poverty stricken people around Cambodia accepted Jesus as Savior year after year. Sadly, Bobby passed away while doing ministry in Cambodia in early 2009. This was extremely difficult for Setan, because he and Bobby didn't just do ministry together, they were truly brothers in the Lord. Setan plans to continue these evangelistic concert tours as God provides the musicians and the funds for rice in the future.

Setan and Bobby doing rice distribution

~*~*~

Setan's heart for his native people also includes hosting medical mission teams. There are very few of the small villages in Cambodia that have any kind of medical facility, so the need for medical and dental attention is great. This ministry outreach allows the love of Christ to be presented through the expression of medical care to those in desperate need of these services. The people not only receive the medical help, but also are given the gospel of Jesus Christ in various ways. These medical mission teams are generally self funded and provide a cost-effective way to expand the presentation of the Gospel into many outlying villages. These teams are strategically placed to also complement our existing ministries and our churches in the poorest locations.

~*~*~

TransformAsia can certainly attest to the fact that ministry is very rewarding and with many great blessings, but it also includes many disappointments. In the fall of 2007, for the first time in fifteen years of ministry, Setan and Randa were forced to close the Ministries Training Center in Phnom Penh due to lack of funding. They also had to let go about 100 people that were on staff in the various ministries around Cambodia as well. In October that year, Setan wrote, "This has been a heavy burden for both of us as the training of Christian leaders is the strongest desire we have right now. But we are still operating all the other ministries and training pastors as best we can."

At the same time Setan was informing his supporters and prayer partners of this situation, TransformAsia was hosting a Pastor's

Conference in Phnom Penh of about 250 pastors from TA churches and many other denominations from all over Cambodia. The Church on the Ridge in Snoqualmie (near Seattle, Washington) financially sponsored this conference and provided pastors and leaders for it. This was a great boost to the work in their churches and ministries, and to Setan and Randa. Even as they closed their Ministry Training Center, they knew God was still providing much needed training in a new way.

In this same October correspondence, Setan stated that the board realized that if they were going to expand TA's ministries in Cambodia, they had to find a way to increase their financial base. He explained their plan to accomplish this.

TA felt that they truly needed to find someone to man an office in the Denver area. They needed someone to help with fund-raising, bookkeeping, administrative assistance, and help write promotional materials. From the founding of the ministry, most of the administrative work had been done by very capable volunteers. However, they were not available to answer phones, provide information to inquirers, and help do Setan and

Randa's scheduling, and many other things that were much needed. TA felt that having someone in an office in Denver would be a tremendous help to the entire ministry. They had applied for a grant in hopes to use it for this purpose, but knew the grant would not be forthcoming for at least 8-10 months. So they set their plan in motion and continued to pray.

Amazingly, God provided for the TransformAsia office right away. Faith Presbyterian Church in Aurora, CO, came along side Setan and Randa once again by providing them office space in their church. Then in January 2008, God answered their prayers by providing a woman to assist in that office. He also sent a very capable woman who was elected to the TransformAsia Treasurer position. The two women worked closely together to organize and establish procedures for the new office. This office has become a very busy place and is the hub of much of TransformAsia's operations.

In August that year, a fundraising banquet was held at a local hotel. Not only did this banquet raise much needed funds, but it met the requirements for the matching grant TransformAsia had applied for in the previous year. God again had provided the needs of the ministry! To God be all the Glory, now and forever!

Chapter 17

MULTIPLIED BLESSINGS

૮ફ્ટે૦

IN 2003, SETAN AND RANDA PUR-
chased farm land in northwest Cambodia
where they could grow rice to help feed the
children and young people God had entrusted
to their care. Eventually, they realized that
a little town near there was filled with close
to 300 children who were at extreme risk of
exploitation. The town is Kambour Village.
It offered very few employment opportunities, so most of the parents of these children
left them in the care of older siblings, or an
elderly grandmother, and went into Thailand
to look for any type of work they could get.
Sadly, few of them have returned to the village, leaving their children at great risk. The
older children and elderly grandmothers have

almost no resources to feed and clothe these children.

Setan and the TransformAsia Board began to work toward a sponsorship program to help them take care of these children. They truly did not have the resources to take care of all these children any other way. Their purpose was to prevent these precious children being kidnapped or sold into the sex trade. It was a huge task and TransformAsia did all they could to protect and feed these children.

In early 2008, the need for more sponsors became paramount. They published this need on the TA website and letters were mailed to TA partners to present the plight of these children. The response has been good, but many more sponsors are still needed. Seeing these children come for the meals that are being provided by TA, and for medical attention when it is provided, is a tremendous joy, but yet it tears at the heart. The need is so great and TA can only partially fill the needs of all these children at this time. TA is praying for God to supply the means to drill a deep well for clean water and to build a huge community center with a kitchen, dinning area, and toilet facilities. They believe that God will provide for these precious ones!

~*~*~

Stung Meanchey Municipal Waste Dump is located in southern Phnom Penh. It is in a part of the city where there are very poor people living in slums. It covers close to 100 acres and is nearly 100 feet high. Next to it is private property where rubbish pickers build huts and are charged very high rents by the land-owners. Those that can't afford the rent end up living on the edges of the dump itself, mostly in cardboard shacks. There are about 2,000 people who live there and about 600 of them are children.

"Smoky Mountain" is its nickname because of the smoke that the dump continually exudes. As the waste rots, it creates methane. Especially in the monsoon season and much of the rest of the year, the area around it becomes flooded. The children live and play in this contaminated water. About 100 of the children are preschool age and are there with their parents or other relatives who work or live on the dump.

In mid-2008, Crossroads Television in Canada began working with TransformAsia by sponsoring a refuge for these preschool children. A rental facility was obtained a short distance from the dump to accommodate a program that will serve approximately 40 children per day. They have a director at the refuge that works with four nannies (caretakers), two cooks, and a van driver to pick up children and transport food and supplies. It is called the *Joy Day Care.*

After the children are picked up in the morning and arrive at JDC, they are immediately given baths and put into clean clothing. They are given a good meal and taught pre-school level educational activities that will expose the children and their families to the Gospel of Jesus and prepare the children to enter elementary school. They are also given snacks before they are returned to their parents or relatives.

TransformAsia brings in nurses about once a month to give medical checkups for the children and provide medicine and medical attention as needed. Only our Heavenly Father knows the true needs of each of these people. The Joy Day Care claims the truth of Psalm 72:4

"He will defend the afflicted among the people and save the children of the needy; he will crush the oppressor." (NIV)

~*~*~

A great number of short term mission teams come to work with TransformAsia in their various ministries. One of the favorite places of these teams is the David Center Orphanage in Anlong Veng. The children in that orphanage are so precious and love to have people visit them. They love hugs and their smiles will capture your heart! Every mission team member who comes to David Center is not only a blessing to the children, but the children bless them too, with their smiles and songs of praise. Within a few years, these children will be young Christian adults and Setan and Randa pray that they will go out and teach and preach to more people about our Lord, and that they will be able to help build the infrastructure of their country.

~*~*~

Some of the short term mission teams that are made up of mostly women enjoy going to the New Development Center (Women's Center) to minister to the young ladies and encourage them. Many of these young girls have been rescued from brothels, or from the enslavement of pimps. Some have come from brutal home lives, frequently having been left with relatives after their parents died. Their stories are hard to listen to.

For example, Chenda and Sila's father died of a demonic cure that a local Witch doctor gave him just after their younger brothers were born. They had lived on a farm, but it had been sold before their father's death to pay for the expensive treatments he was given. After his death they were sent to live with their aunt in another city.

The aunt was very hard on the children, making them work at many different jobs. She allowed Chenda to attend school until she was in the 5th grade, but then she was made to drop out of school. However, Sila and her younger brothers were not allowed schooling and were illiterate.

They did very hard labor for the aunt and when they didn't meet her expectations, she beat them mercilessly many, many times. The aunt became so exasperated with the seemingly unprofitable girls that she finally sold them. The man who purchased them was the owner of a local restaurant where the girls were made to sit next to the customers and allow them to touch them inappropriately.

The girls were extremely traumatized, and refused to comply with the owner's expectations. He tried to force them to do as he said, but amazingly, they were able to escape. As they ran from the restaurant, they ran into a lady on the street and asked her for help.

The woman was the counselor and Bible teacher at TA's New Development Center for rescued women. She told them that they could be given a new home and a new life. As she explained this to them, they were overjoyed and moved into the center immediately. There, Chenda studied sewing and Sila studied cosmetology. They were hoping to find a new life for themselves with these new professions. Both girls received Christ as Savior after they came to the center, so they will also have eternal life with Jesus!

Girls and young women continue to come through the women's center year after year. More than 98% of them come to know Jesus as Savior during their stay. To Setan and Randa, this is the most important truth they want these ladies to take with them as they graduate from their training at the New Development Center.

~*~*~

As Setan and Randa Lee continue to follow God's plan for their lives in Cambodia, they have found that God's call on their lives is not short term. Their work continues as they reach into more and more areas of the country where people are starving spiritually and physically. Christianity is still in the minority by far, and poverty is still extremely wide spread. They have made many in-roads into the country's problems, but they still dream of more ways to lead people to Jesus and to help rebuild the infrastructure of Cambodia.

It is also their prayer that each team member or visitor who comes to Cambodia to work with their ministries will catch the vision God has given them and become long term partners in their work.

Setan and Randa also pray that if you are reading this book and do not know Jesus, the Lord of this Universe, as your personal Savior, that you will take the time now to ask Him into your heart and life. It is the most important thing you will ever do, and eternal life with Jesus is yours for the taking. Just take the following steps:

**(1) Realize that you are a sinner in need of a Savior (Romans 3:23, *For all have* *sinned and fall short of the glory of God.)*

(2) Know the cost of a sinful life. (Romans 6:23, *For the wages of sins is death, but the gift of God is eternal life in Christ Jesus our Lord.)*

(3) See God's provision and love. (Romans 5:8, *But God demonstrates his own love for us in this: while we were still sinners, Christ died for us.)*

(4) Ask Jesus to come into your heart. (Romans 10:9-10, *That if you confess with your month, "Jesus is Lord," and believe in your heart that God raised Him from the dead, you will be saved. For it is with your heart that you believe and are justified, and it is with your month that you confess and are saved.)*

(5) Accept the assurance of your salvation. (St. John 1: 12-13, *...to all who received Him, to those who believed in His name, he gave the right to become children of God – children born not of natural descent, nor of human decision or a husband's will, but born of God."*

** All scriptures taken from the NIV.

If you have accepted Jesus as your Savior, please let someone know. Transform-Asia would like to hear from you. You can contact the office in Aurora. See the end of this book for our contact information. You need to publicly confess your faith in Jesus as Lord and get together with others who know Jesus and grow together in His Word and in His Power! God bless you and keep you always.

~*~*~

The impact of the ministries of Setan and Randa Lee on their homeland, and on every person that has the privilege of working with them, or reading about them, is yet to be known. It is their calling from God the Father to take the hope and love of Jesus Christ to the people of Cambodia, and others they come in contact with along the way. They will continue their work until God tells them to stop, or until He calls them to their reward in Heaven. It is certain that they will witness many more miracles in that forgotten land!

The Lee Family

EPILOGUE

꧁꧂

A S *MIRACLES IN THE FORGOTTEN LAND AND BEYOND* was being readied for publication, a Canadian man telephoned Setan Lee and said that he had been reading about TransformAsia's Cambodian ministries and wanted to ask some questions about the work. He and Setan talked for almost two hours. During this conversation, he asked Setan, "What is the greatest need you have there right now?"

After a little thought, Setan told him about the many children in Kambour Village and their great needs. He explained that the children desperately need clean water for drinking and cooking and that TransformAsia needs to drill a deep well there as soon as possible. He also told him that if TA could build a large community center in Kambour with a kitchen and dining area, they could prepare meals and feed many more children. (Currently, they can feed only about 40 children at a time because of the tiny space they have to work in, and because they only have enough dishes for that many. They have to wash the dishes between shifts of feeding the children.) The gentleman listened intently. Then he suggested that perhaps they would need toilet facilities as well. Setan agreed that this too was much needed. Then the man asked Setan about the cost of providing all of this in Kambour.

To Setan's amazement, the man told him that he would mail a check right away to cover all these expenses! God is so great! *We praise Him for bringing this wonderful servant in the Kingdom of God along side the ministries of TransformAsia.*

God has also called a young minister and his wife to become the Directors of the David Center Orphanage in Anlong Veng. They plan to arrive there in late summer of 2010. This is a tremendous answer to prayer. Randa spent seven months filling this position which had been vacant for a while before she arrived there. She and Setan both need to be able to carry on their work in all their ministries; it is difficult for either of them to fill a vacated position for very long. So this young couple will be a great blessing and answer to prayer as they arrive at the David Center to direct the care and ministry of about 60 orphans.

Discussions are underway between this new Director at David Center Orphanage and some business men on the West coast about sponsoring the orphanage center either monthly or quarterly. Who knows what God has planned with these gentlemen?

God has blessed TransformAsia with a number of people who have been able to provide the resources for large projects that He wanted done for His Glory. Some of them are continuing to bless TA with their generosity and prayers. However, the TA board feels that God is also telling them to reach out, because He has even greater things that need to be accomplished. They know that God has given them a plan for this. That plan is to find many people who will give a little so that much more can be accomplished for His glory in the foreseeable future. They have begun working to launch this plan. It is a sponsorship program that will provide resources for the basic foundation for the work God continually lays before TransformAsia.

Setan and Randa are praying that people who read their story in this book or on their web site, and see the work God is doing in Cambodia and the surrounding area, will consider becoming friends and prayer partners with TransformAsia. They need to reach the millions that are still unreached in Cambodia and all of Southeast Asia.

If you feel God is placing this ministry on your heart, please go to the web site and become one of the sponsors of the TransformAsia ministries. God is still doing great miracles among His people around the world! The sponsorships are only $39 per month and you can designate the area you want TA to use your funds.

(1) Women's Ministries (the Women's Center and Trade School): Help Setan and Randa as they bring more and more children and young girls out of the sex trade and into a home for restoration and to hear the Gospel as they learn new skills.

(2) The David Center Orphanage: TA continually brings more orphaned and abandoned children off the streets and out of harms way, and teaches them

the Love of Jesus as they care for them. Children from birth to teenagers are brought into the orphanage to give them a home and a better future.

(3) Kambour Village: Help TA bring some stability into this village and provide so the children can go to school and enable TA to teach them the Gospel of Jesus and His saving Grace. With almost 300 children looking to TransformAsia for help, the need is great and will continue for many years. It remains to be seen how God will lead as TA reaches out in this village.

(4) Cambodia's first Christian University: Plans are going forward to get the TransformAsia Christian University built. TA is trusting God for $5,000,000 for this project over the next 5 years. Pray for this much needed University to become a reality for the Glory of God!

WILL YOU JOIN IN THE WORK WITH SETAN AND RANDA LEE WITH A MONTHLY SPONSORSHIP OF $39? You can do this by going to www.transformasia. us to set up your monthly donation. May God richly bless you as you make this decision to become a partner with Setan and Randa Lee in their work.

They truly believe that God has a plan for their lives and for everyone who has a relationship with the Lord Jesus Christ. They are confident that those plans are for good, and that they definitely have a great future and a blessed hope in Jesus. They believe that God has a plan for the ministries of TransformAsia and that He will bless these ministries and bring His plans to fruition.

Randa and Setan Lee are the Co-founders and leaders of **Kampuchea for Christ, dba TransformAsia, Inc.** The ministry in the United States is headquartered in Aurora, Colorado, and their Asia headquarters is in Phnom Penh, Cambodia. They have truly been brought a long way from the Killing Fields of Cambodia to the amazing life of service for the Lord of the Universe! But they still lean heavily on God's promise that is found in Jeremiah 29:11:

"For I know the plans I have for you," *declares the Lord, "plans to prosper you and* *not to harm you, plans to give you hope and* *a future." (NIV)*

Setan Lee is the President and CEO of TransformAsia. He and the Board of Directors are diligently praying and working to know and follow God's guidance as they lead the ministries of TransformAsia into the future. Randa Lee is the Director of Women's Ministries and also helps oversee the David Center Orphanage. Many things are still happening that can only come from the miraculous hands of God as He works in and through Setan and Randa's lives.

Just as God miraculously brought Setan and Randa through the killing fields of Cambodia, they believe that this same God will also work miracles in your life as you seek His counsel and guidance in your life's journey.

John 16:24 (NKJV), *Until now you have asked nothing in My name. Ask, and you will receive, that your joy may be full.*

CONTACT INFORMATION

If you would like to have Dr. Setan Aaron Lee speak at your church or other venues, please contact TransformAsia. Frequently, Randa is able to join Setan as he speaks in various places around the world.

Address:
TransformAsia
P.O. Box 440283
Aurora, CO
80044-0283

Email addresses:
info@transformasia.us (Office)
slee@transformasia.us (Setan)
rlee@transformasia.us (Randa)

Office phone: 303-693-6122

Web Site: www.transformasia.us

*Angkor Wat (*Near Siem Reap)

FACTS ABOUT CAMBODIA

❧

The country is called the Kingdom of Cambodia; also know as "Kampuchea."

Location: In South East Asia, bordering the Gulf of Thailand, between Thailand, Vietnam, and Laos.

Area: 69,884 Square miles) About the size of the state of Missouri in the United States.

Population: 14 million with a growth rate of about 2.5% annually.

Climate: Tropical: rainy, monsoon season (May to November); dry season (December to April); little seasonal temperature variation.

Terrain: Mostly low, flat plains; mountains in the southwest and north.

Capital City: Phnom Penh with a population of over one million.

Government: Constitutional Monarchy

Language: Khmer (the official language), French, and English

Ethnicity: 90% Khmer, 5% Vietnamese, 1% Chinese, 4% Other

Religions: 95% Theravada Buddhist, 5% Other

Literacy Rate: 69%

Natural Resources: Timber, gemstones, some iron ore, manganese, phosphates, hydropower potential.